ORTHO'S All About

Home Offices

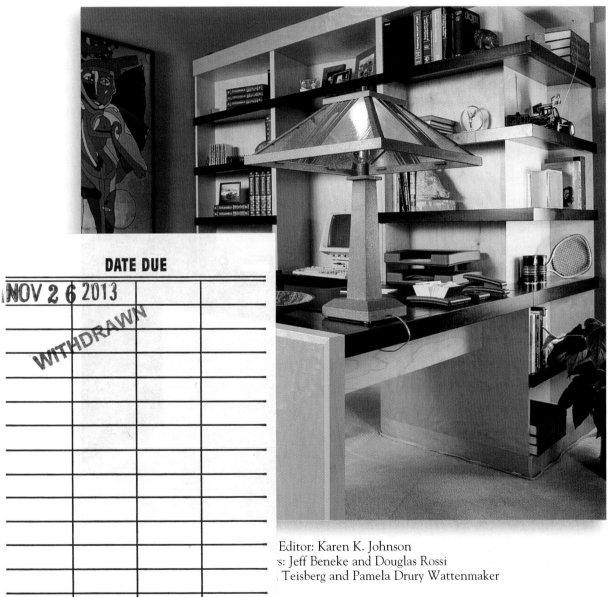

Editor: Karen K. Johnson
s: Jeff Beneke and Douglas Rossi
Teisberg and Pamela Drury Wattenmaker

Meredith® Books
Des Moines, Iowa

Ortho® Books
An imprint of Meredith® Books

Ortho's All About Home Offices
Solaris Book Development Team
Publisher: Robert B. Loperena
Editorial Director: Christine Jordan
Managing Editor: Sally W. Smith
Acquisitions Editors: Robert J. Beckstrom,
    Michael D. Smith
Publisher's Assistant: Joni Christiansen
Graphics Coordinator: Sally J. French
Editorial Coordinator: Cass Dempsey
Production Manager: Linda Bouchard

Meredith Book Development Team
Editor: Larry Erickson
Art Director: Tom Wegner
Copy Chief: Catherine Hamrick
Copy and Production Editor: Terri Fredrickson
Contributing Copy Editor: Steve Marlens
Contributing Proofreader: Colleen Johnson
Indexer: Donald Glassman
Electronic Production Coordinator: Paula Forest
Editorial and Design Assistants: Kathleen Stevens,
    Judy Bailey, Kaye Chabot, Treesa Landry, Karen Schirm
Production Director: Douglas M. Johnston
Production Manager: Pam Kvitne
Assistant Prepress Manager: Marjorie J. Schenkelberg

Additional Editorial Contributions from
    Art Rep Services
Director: Chip Nadeau
Designer: Laura Rades
Illustrator: John Teisberg

Meredith® Books
Editor in Chief: James D. Blume
Design Director: Matt Strelecki
Managing Editor: Gregory H. Kayko
Executive Ortho Editor: Benjamin W. Allen

Director, Sales & Marketing, Retail: Michael A. Peterson
Director, Sales & Marketing, Special Markets:
    Rita McMullen
Director, Sales & Marketing, Home & Garden Center
    Channel: Ray Wolf
Director, Operations: George A. Susral

Vice President, General Manager: Jamie L. Martin

Meredith Publishing Group
President, Publishing Group: Christopher M. Little
Vice President, Consumer Marketing & Development:
    Hal Oringer

Meredith Corporation
Chairman and Chief Executive Officer: William T. Kerr

Chairman of the Executive Committee: E.T. Meredith III

Photographers
Laurie Black: 10, 76R
Kim Brun: 8
Stephen Cridland: 50T
Peter Christiansen/California Redwood Association: 85B
DeGennaro Associates: cover, 4, 20T, 20B, 51T
Susan Gilmore: 50B
Edward Gohlich: 6T, 30
Jay Graham: 66, 86
Bob Hawks: 14, 62T
Hedrich-Blessing Studios: 61, 78, 82, 84T
William Hopkins Sr.: 59
Jon Jensen: 35
Michael Jensen: 7, 9, 76L
D. Livingston: 51B, 55, 68
David O. Marlow: 19
Barbara Martin: 85T
Tom McWilliam: 6B
Timothy Murphy: 52
Kenneth Rice: 64T, 64B
William Stites: 62B
Bryan Whitney: 84B
James Yokum: 80

All of us at Ortho® Books are dedicated to providing you
with the information and ideas you need to enhance your
home and garden. We welcome your comments and
suggestions about this book. Write to us at:
    Meredith Corporation
    Ortho Books
    1716 Locust St.
    Des Moines, IA 50309–3023

Note to the Readers: Due to differing conditions, tools,
and individual skills, Meredith Corporation assumes no
responsibility for any damages, injuries suffered, or losses
incurred as a result of following the information published
in this book. Before beginning any project, review the
instructions carefully, and if any doubts or questions remain,
consult local experts or authorities. Because codes and
regulations vary greatly, you always should check with
authorities to ensure that your project complies with all
applicable local codes and regulations. Always read and
observe all of the safety precautions provided by
manufacturers of any tools, equipment, or supplies,
and follow all accepted safety procedures.

Ortho® is a trademark of Monsanto Company used
under license.

PLANNING A HOME OFFICE   4

HOME OFFICE DESIGN   14

BUILDING SKILLS   30

DOUBLE IDENTITY   52

CONVERTING SPACE   64

ADDING SPACE   82

In this home office, an English armoire with burled maple doors provides storage and style. The desk is simple— file cabinets covered with a glass-topped, hollow-core door.

PLANNING A HOME OFFICE

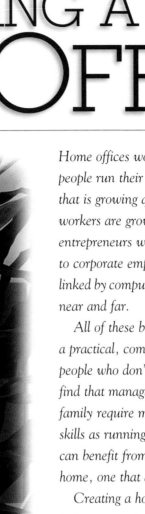

Home offices work. That's why more and more people run their business from home, a trend that is growing quickly. Categories of home workers are growing, too, from freelance entrepreneurs who run their own businesses to corporate employees who telecommute, linked by computer networks with coworkers near and far.

All of these businesses share one basic need: a practical, comfortable workspace. And even people who don't work at home professionally find that managing a household and raising a family require many of the same organizational skills as running a small business. They, too, can benefit from an efficient office space at home, one that all family members can use.

Creating a home office is unlike other home-improvement projects because the goal is not only to make your home more comfortable and attractive, but also to define a space that is critical to the income of the household.

However, you should be aware that home offices raise a variety of unique legal, financial, and work-related issues. This chapter presents some of the points to consider before you act.

THE ELECTRONIC WORKPLACE

The personal computer has touched just about every aspect of our lives. But perhaps no facet of human activity has been so dramatically affected as our work. Both the nature of the work and the sites where we conduct it have undergone rapid alterations. So many people are working at home today, full-time and part-time, that the real estate and construction fields have christened a new room of the house: the home office. In new home construction and remodeling, in large houses and small, people are configuring rooms to accommodate their work.

Though small, this home office is efficient. It has cubbyholes for office supplies, twin file cabinets, a flip-down desktop, and fluorescent work light.

Of course, every home already has some form of office, whether it's called that or not. It may be a kitchen drawer, a desk in the family room, or an entire room. But these offices are often afterthoughts and don't meet today's needs.

Studies show that home offices grow in stages: Most home offices start out on the dining room table, in a kitchen cabinet, or in a drawer. Then the papers and clutter overflow onto the floor. Next, paperwork makes its way into the living room, which can be reclaimed only by designating some other room as the office (outfitting it with furniture and equipment purchased on an as-needed basis). The result? The "office" is an eclectic mix of questionable style and dubious function—not to mention a tangle of extension cords. That cycle needs to be broken. By thinking through and planning your home office, you will keep your business in business.

COMFORT AND EFFICIENCY

Planning a home office involves more than making room for a desk and chair. You want a work environment that maximizes efficiency, productivity, and comfort. If clients will visit your home office, you'll need an entrance that does not compromise the privacy of your family. Most people want an office that can be sealed off from the rest of the house, with soundproofing to keep house noises from disrupting work and vice versa.

A well-designed home office must be wired for a variety of electronic office tools; wiring should include phone lines to handle fax, modem, and conventional calls. Your office should be a place in which you feel comfortable and enjoy working. And it should enhance the value and appearance of your largest investment—your home.

Making a home office may require little more than rearranging a room, or it may entail a major renovation. If you just can't find the space for an office in your current floor plan, you may need to construct an addition. Whatever the scope of the work, this book helps you through the process step by step.

Tucked in a closet, this 4½×12-foot office was outfitted to meet the needs of a work-at-home designer. When the workday is over, she closes the doors on the clutter.

WORK AND HOME LIFE UNDER ONE ROOF

When you commute to a job, the division between work and home life is clearly defined. Once you start working out of a home office, that separation becomes less clear and can cause problems. For some, the purpose of a home office is to centralize the operation of a household, while for others it revolves around a business. For most people, however, a new home office must accommodate both functions.

YOUR FAMILY, INC.

Even if you don't telecommute or earn income out of your home, you still are running a vital business: Your Family, Inc. You perform many of the same functions as a Fortune 500 corporation. You pay bills (accounts payable department). You take in paychecks, stock dividends, interest, and other income (accounts receivable). Every year, you prepare detailed financial statements (tax returns). There are stockholder meetings (family discussions), business proposals (job applications), and so on.

Of course, it's simpler and cheaper to set up an office to handle the family business than to set up a design studio or landscaping service. But you'll benefit in the long run if you strive for big-business efficiency in the operation of your home office.

The organizational tips and techniques in this book help you keep track of the bills, taxes, warranty cards, instruction manuals, and other paperwork required in a modern household. When things are organized, finding them isn't a chore, and dealing with them is less likely to be put off. Who has the willpower to search through boxes of unorganized records for a missing receipt?

After you've chosen a location for the paperwork, the next step is to label everything clearly, then let others know how it is organized. That way, if the person who usually handles certain paperwork is away, another person can step in.

When setting up your own office, you also can seize the opportunity to teach older children how to handle their papers and affairs, how to set up a basic filing system, and how to label items. This will be helpful in the future when they encounter the insurance documents, car titles, tax records, and other paperwork of "the real world."

ESTABLISHING BOUNDARIES

When your home office exists mainly to generate income, you must decide how much overlap with everyday home life you will allow.

Often, the office computer is the biggest obstacle to maintaining a private working environment. That's because computers are not just work tools for adults. Loaded with the right software and accessories, today's home computer is a sophisticated toy, a research and educational tool, and a popular diversion for every member of the family. Today's children with access to a computer spend less time surfing television channels and more time surfing the Internet.

As computer prices continue to fall, many find it possible to dedicate one computer to office use and another to the household. If you are not prepared to make that investment, think carefully about how to manage the many competing demands for computer time.

A busy family needs a home management center. This one is tucked into a corner between the kitchen and the family room.

YOUR OFFICE AS AN INVESTMENT

Any investment you make in a home office will affect the value of your house. It makes a lot of sense, therefore, to take that into consideration before you start building. Because of the popularity of home offices, you may discover that spending a little more on the project now may reap bigger returns down the road when you sell your house. Conversely, a poorly planned, low-budget approach to building the home office today may come back to haunt you.

INVESTING IN AN OFFICE

Fortunately, you don't have to be rich to make your office look and feel professional. Although creating a professional and workable space does take an investment, it need not be exorbitant. And, if done correctly, it can even improve your work.

How much does a home office cost? As much or as little as you want. A desk, file cabinet, good chair, and basic office necessities cost from a few hundred to several thousand dollars. The expense of customizing a room for a home office depends on how much remodeling is needed.

When deciding how much to spend on furnishings, consider how long the office will be used—a few years or the rest of your career? When deciding how much to spend on remodeling, consider how long you plan to stay in the house. If you think it will be on the market in a year, ask yourself whether it pays to make major renovations.

Be forewarned that even homeowners with the most carefully planned budgets often discover that costs run higher than planned. It's wise to add 20–30 percent to your estimate so you are less likely to be surprised by unexpected expenses after the work begins. And, in the pleasant event that you run under budget, you can pocket the excess or use it to buy better furniture and equipment.

If you'll be telecommuting—working at home for a remote employer—your company may be willing to provide some of the furnishings and equipment. A growing part of the office furniture business is selling equipment to companies setting up their employees at home. By submitting a budget and showing how you can be more productive at home, you may be able to persuade your company to pay for the equipment you need.

INVESTING IN YOUR HOUSE

Try to approach a home office project as you would any other home improvement. Design it to complement the style of your house. Use materials that are likely to hold up. And, most important, think about how a future owner might want to use the space. If you're building an addition or doing a major renovation, make the space functional as an office *and* easily convertible to another use, should the office no longer be needed by the next owner.

Snuggled into the heart of the home, this work station features a big interior window looking out over the family room and kitchen. Panes of glass block out family-room noise. Built-in drawers maximize storage, and the lowered platform for the keyboard eases the strain of long work sessions.

HOME OFFICES AND TAXES

In figuring your budget, consider the potential tax deduction of expenses for home office furniture and improvements. You may be able to deduct such costs from your business income. Conditions vary, and the rules change frequently, so check the current tax codes with an accountant.

DEDUCTIONS FOR EQUIPMENT PURCHASES

You may qualify to deduct the cost of equipment, furniture, and improvements for your home office. For example, a writer who produces work at home and delivers it electronically may qualify for a deduction, whereas a plumber who works in other locations, despite keeping records and billing materials at home and storing equipment there, may not. If you qualify, your desk and file cabinets may be deductible expenses.

DEFINING A HOME OFFICE

Your definition of a home office may differ substantially from the Internal Revenue Service's. Many people who work at home do not claim home office deductions because they fear triggering a tax audit. Such caution can be costly. Allowable deductions on a home office can add up to thousands of dollars a year.

Generally, you can claim a deduction if you conduct most of your business at home. You must use the office space regularly and exclusively for work-related activities. For many businesses, that means you must meet clients regularly at your home office.

If your house qualifies as your principal place of business, you are entitled to deductions for the purchase of computers, office furniture, and other equipment. To meet this requirement, you must:
■ Spend more time working at home than anywhere else.
■ Generate more income from work in the home office than from any other source.
■ Use the home office regularly and exclusively for work.

For more details, call 800/829-3676 to order IRS Publication 587, "Business Use of Your Home." For specific questions, look in your telephone directory under United States Government, Internal Revenue Service, Federal Tax Information. Or call the IRS referral line, 800/829-1040.

DEDUCTIONS FOR HOUSING COSTS

You may be entitled to deduct a portion of the costs of utilities, insurance, rent, mortgage interest, and taxes, based on the size of your office in relation to the total area of the house. For example, let's say you have a 100-square-foot office in a home with a total of 2,000 square feet. Heat, electricity, insurance, mortgage interest, and property taxes add up to $11,000 a year. Because 100 square feet represents 5 percent of the total area, your deduction would be $550 (5 percent of $11,000).

DEPRECIATING SPACE AND EQUIPMENT

Cars used for business can be depreciated, as can software and, in certain circumstances, business hardware. If you are a homeowner, you also are allowed to depreciate the amount of space dedicated to the home office.

Be advised, however, that using the depreciation deduction, however, can be complicated. It can work for or against you, because it may affect what's called the "basis" of your home and may mean higher taxes later if you show a profit on the sale. Determining the correct "basis" may mean hiring an appraiser and having all the receipts for improvements and repairs to the property. You also may need the help of an accountant in figuring out the correct depreciation.

When you sell your home, the tax law may allow an exemption for the portion of your home used for business, provided it is converted back to personal use the year before you sell. Again, it's wise to check with an accountant.

Filled with yarn samples, paints, family photos, and the requisite office gear, this studio is a creative sanctuary.

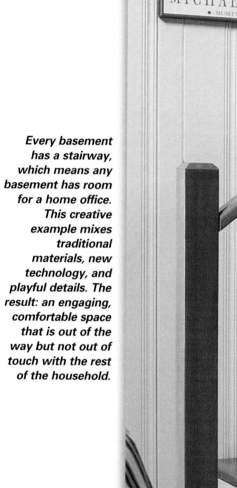

Every basement has a stairway, which means any basement has room for a home office. This creative example mixes traditional materials, new technology, and playful details. The result: an engaging, comfortable space that is out of the way but not out of touch with the rest of the household.

KEEPING IT LEGAL: ZONING AND PERMITS

Before you get started on your home office, you may need permission from the local zoning agency to operate a home-based business. In addition, many building projects require permits.

ZONING

Zoning is usually not a problem if you are a freelancer working alone. However, if you engage in certain types of commerce, you may be operating a commercial enterprise within a residentially zoned area, and zoning does become an issue.

Problems also may arise if you have a business sign on the property, have lots of visitors, hire employees, store business items in plain sight, or have neighbors who complain about your business activities.

To avoid inspections by local officials and possible citations, thoroughly research your town's rules governing home offices. At your town hall, city hall, or county offices, you can find out from the zoning or planning department which home occupations are permitted under the zoning law. Request a copy of the pertinent zoning regulations.

If your intended use is not permitted, you can seek a variance, which may mean petitioning the zoning board to hold a public hearing. Also, be aware that certain condominiums and housing developments have restrictive covenants limiting home offices in their deeds or association bylaws.

BUILDING PERMITS

If you plan to construct an addition or remodel a garage for your office, you will probably need a building permit. Where the office will be used by the entire family, the space would be described merely as "additional living space" on the permit application; more elaborate offices may be subject to a variety of local requirements. If you are a physician, for example, and want to build an addition with a separate entrance for your practice, you may be required to add a separate bathroom for patients and provide off-street parking. In such a case, renting commercial space may be more economical.

Local building codes follow national models, but there can be local variations. Usually, a permit is needed when renovations are structural and change the size or use of living space. Building a closet or adding a partition wall doesn't usually require a permit (but some communities may require one, so check). Dormers and additions need permits because the alterations change the structure and exterior appearance of the house. Plans for those projects should be reviewed and approved by an architect or structural engineer.

Permits ensure that work is inspected and meets safety standards. They also reduce the possibility that an insurance company will cite faulty work as a cause of subsequent damage or fire.

Setbacks limit how close you can build to your property's boundaries. In this example, the home is positioned as close as allowed to the front and one side boundary. Expansion can only occur to the other side or to the back of the house.

DO IT YOURSELF?

One of your biggest decisions is whether to hire professionals, do the work yourself, or do certain parts yourself and hire contractors for the rest.

Begin with an honest assessment of your own skills and capabilities. Are you handy with tools and knowledgeable about basic construction? Can you work quickly enough to have the office up and running when you need it? Do you have time for such a project, or would it be more efficient to have a contractor supply the heavy labor so you can concentrate on generating income?

JOBS FOR A CONTRACTOR

If you are a part-time do-it-yourselfer, there are skills it probably doesn't pay for you to learn. Work involving plumbing, electrical wiring, mechanical systems, and foundations may require a permit and regular inspections. If you hire a contractor for these jobs, it is the contractor's responsibility to meet code requirements. If you do the work yourself and it fails to pass inspection, the additional cost comes straight out of your pocket.

If you decide to hire someone, get references. The best references come by word of mouth from friends and neighbors. Before selecting any contractor:

■ Ask for and follow up on three references.
■ Check with the Better Business Bureau to see whether the contractor has any adverse records on file.
■ Ask for bank references.
■ Make sure the contractor is properly bonded or licensed and adequately insured.

CONTRACTS

If you decide to use a contractor, you need a contract. A good contract includes these details (some may not pertain to your situation):

■ References to construction documents, including site plans, working drawings, and the written description of the scope of work. For small jobs, a description of the work and quality of materials will do.
■ A payment schedule. Request staggered payments, such as a third at the start, a third halfway through, and the last third at completion after the building inspector's okay.
■ The contractor's certificate of insurance covering all risks.
■ A stipulation that the contractor obtain necessary permits, perform the work to code, and get necessary inspections.

■ Startup and completion dates. When the work is completed, inspected, and approved, get a signed receipt and a lien release. Also for lien releases from the contractor's suppliers to ensure they've been paid for the materials used on the job.

TYPICAL HOMEOWNER PROJECTS FOR A NEW HOME OFFICE

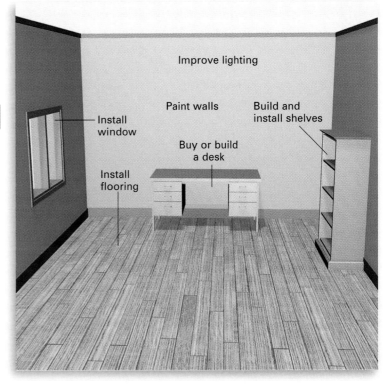

Improve lighting

Paint walls

Build and install shelves

Install window

Buy or build a desk

Install flooring

TASKS BETTER SUITED TO A PROFESSIONAL BUILDER

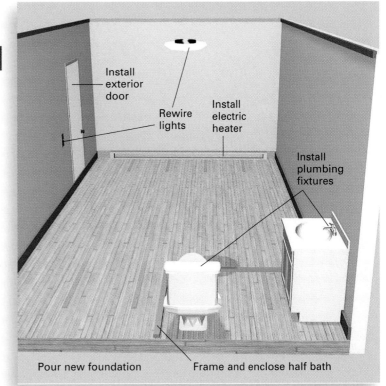

Install exterior door

Rewire lights

Install electric heater

Install plumbing fixtures

Pour new foundation   Frame and enclose half bath

In a former life, this colorful office was a dining room. By filling the space with a collection of textiles and folk art, the work room is transformed into a friendly retreat. Partitions offer out-of-the-way display spots. Shelving resembles adobe niches to fit in with the room's motif.

HOME OFFICE DESIGN

When you walk into an office, the furniture, layout, and equipment tell you a lot about the people who work there and the kind of work they do. The most impressive offices balance inventive use of space with tasteful furnishings. Achieving this balance requires an artful touch, as well as an understanding of the elements needed for an efficient work environment.

First, you need to decide whether you can find a suitable space for your office within your home as it currently exists or whether you need to create new space. If your work involves visits from clients or co-workers, you need to plan for their access to the office.

Comfort and productivity are helped by good furniture arranged wisely. Also, the importance of proper lighting is too often overlooked in the planning stages. The solution is seldom as simple as adding more lamps and bigger bulbs; a good plan balances specific types of electric light with natural light.

This chapter offers ideas that help you design a comfortable, practical work space that meets your needs and budget.

FINDING SPACE

Fine homes built in the 19th century often contained a formal room designated as a den or library—the home office of bygone days. Today, it is the rare home that has a space readily available for, much less designed for, a home office. With a little planning, however, almost any part of a home can be turned into an office. You can:

BORROW SPACE from an existing area, such as a spare bedroom, enclosed porch, or basement. Obviously, this is less costly than constructing something new.

CLAIM SPACE under the stairs, in an alcove, or in a walk-in closet. The resulting cubbyhole office works well for people who need only minimal space. The key to using this type of office effectively is finding storage in the limited space.

CREATE SPACE by building an addition, adding an attic dormer or a bay window, remodeling a garage, or constructing a shed. If the remodeling is structural, you need a building permit. Structural work usually involves moving load-bearing walls, building a foundation, or altering a roof. Putting a shed on your property also may require a permit and may be subject to zoning regulations.

Your minimal space requirements depend on how you intend to use the office.

SHARE SPACE in the kitchen, living room, or bedroom. There are pros and cons to this idea. Many home office consultants advise separating personal and work space, but much depends on how and when the space is used. Sharing space may demand diplomatic skills and the ability to juggle work assignments to accommodate competing needs for the space.

MOVE SPACE around the house or to the car. Your office can be as small and portable as a well-equipped briefcase or shoulder bag, a rolling cart with wire baskets, or a small table on wheels that can be whisked into a closet when not in use. Those who conduct much of their business on the move, such as contractors, landscapers, and sales executives, need a car office with cellular phone and laptop computer, with software to keep appointment files and meeting notes.

SEEKING PROFESSIONAL HELP

To succeed in business, you need to know your strengths and weaknesses. The same is true with a major home renovation. If you are contemplating complex changes, or if you aren't too confident in your own design skills, seek the help of a design professional.

For a large project, consider hiring an architect to make drawings, offer design advice, and prepare specifications. If you plan to have a contractor do some or most of the construction, an architect can help you choose among competitive bids. A growing number of contractors run "design/build" firms, which offer design and construction services.

For smaller projects, seek the advice of an interior decorator, preferably one with experience setting up home offices. Don't overlook the helpful guidance you can get from a consultant who specializes in organizing offices. If you can't find help through word-of-mouth, check your phone directory under Office Planning Services or Interior Decorators and Designers. Office furniture dealers also may be helpful in steering you toward the kind of advice you are seeking.

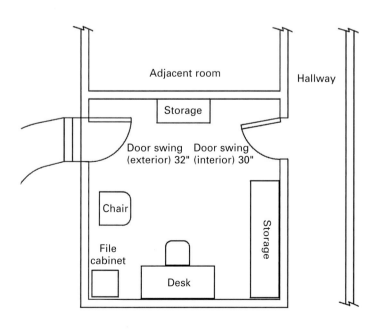

Adjacent room
Hallway
Storage
Door swing   Door swing
(exterior) 32" (interior) 30"
Chair
Storage
File cabinet
Desk

ROOM BY ROOM: SIZING UP POTENTIAL SITES FOR YOUR HOME OFFICE

Room	Pros	Cons
Attic	Attics are often large, unfinished spaces with no territorial claims associated with other rooms in the house. The pitched roof and odd angles provide the opportunity to create a visually interesting environment.	Room height, floor size, and weight load are often big limitations. Providing adequate access can be a problem; stairs must meet strict code requirements. Without adequate insulation, heating, and air conditioning, attics can be uncomfortable in the summer and winter.
Basement	Often one of the least expensive means of creating a private office. Basements usually are out of the flow of household traffic. Basements often are easy to keep warm in winter and cool in summer. And with convenient access to utilities, wiring and other jobs are easier. Basements often have a separate entrance, which is ideal if clients must visit your office.	If the basement is wet, even occasionally, mold and mildew can become a problem for furniture, files, and computers. Height may be too limited for comfort. Basement stairs in older homes frequently do not comply with building codes. Materials stored in the basement will need a new home. Many people may not feel comfortable working in a basement.
Garage	An independent building with a separate entrance. Can be a nonstressful renovation, as the work does not disrupt activities in the house, and the dirt and dust stay in the garage. Expanding over the garage may be an option.	The car must be parked outside, and other stored items may have to be moved. Heating and cooling systems may need to be installed. The office may not be as secure as one inside the house. Ceiling ties may need to be moved higher to allow for adequate headroom.
Kitchen	Many kitchens already function as the de facto home office. They are ideal locations for small offices, if space permits and generally comfortable and well-lighted. Existing cabinets may be used for office storage.	Interruptions and lack of privacy may hinder your work. Proximity to food preparation areas could result in work being affected by spills and stains. If cabinets already are full, storage could be a problem. Evening use may be disruptive.
Bedroom	Private and quiet bedrooms usually are unused during the day. Master bedrooms often are large enough for a small office. Spare bedrooms are the easiest and most popular places for home offices. Utilities, privacy, and a closet already are in place.	Converting a spare bedroom may deprive you of space for overnight guests and storage. A master suite location may crowd your storage and cramp your style. It's difficult for one person to sleep, while another works.
Addition	A new addition can provide all of the room and features you desire in an office without sacrificing space that is being used for other purposes. Or you can build your dream master bedroom with an addition, then turn the vacated bedroom into an office.	Expanding your home can be costly and may require the help of an architect and a builder. Building plans must be submitted for a permit, which can delay construction. Houses on small lots may not allow for an addition that meets local codes.
Separate building	A separate structure offers quiet, privacy, and a separate ground-level entrance. It can be designed and built to meet your specific needs. It can be purchased already built or constructed from scratch.	Security may be compromised, especially if the structure is set in a remote corner of your property. Zoning laws may be too restrictive for a legal structure. Heating and cooling systems will have to be installed, and electricity and phone lines extended.

EVALUATING THE SPACE

Choosing the space that works best for you as an office takes a thorough understanding of your needs.

The first step is to analyze the nature of your work. What are its requirements? Can the space accommodate those needs? For example, if your work requires a computer and peripherals, a cubbyhole office under the stairs may be impractical if the equipment won't fit or get adequate ventilation.

Conversely, it is a waste of space to convert an entire room if all you need is phone and desk space. A family mini-office may require little more than a drawer or a kitchen cabinet with a nearby phone, a file cabinet to store papers, and a work space big enough for spreading out household bills. A corner of the kitchen may be perfect.

You will want your office to be a good neighbor to the rest of the household, so evaluate prospective office space in context. Who and what are in adjacent rooms? How might they affect your ability to work? And how might your work affect them?

It's also important to consider whether you like the space. It can be tough enough to do work; fighting the location doesn't help matters.

In evaluating a space, take into account any physical and structural limitations. These can complicate or prevent the use of many basement, garage, or attic spaces.

POTENTIAL PROBLEMS

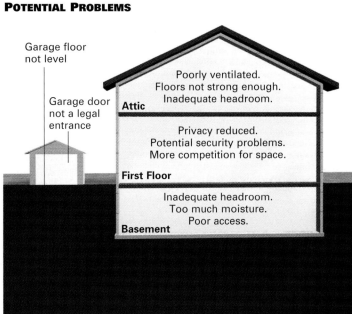

Garage floor not level

Garage door not a legal entrance

Attic
Poorly ventilated.
Floors not strong enough.
Inadequate headroom.

First Floor
Privacy reduced.
Potential security problems.
More competition for space.

Basement
Inadequate headroom.
Too much moisture.
Poor access.

ROOM FOR CHANGE

Your needs for office space can change, so think of the future, too. Will it be possible to modify the space if you have more children; your grown children move out; you acquire more work, larger projects, more equipment; or you need more storage?

Retirement or a change of occupation also may affect your space requirements.

Consider the time frame of such events when weighing the investment that your office will require. You can justify a larger expense if it will serve your needs for many years. The same office investment may be a poor choice if it will be suitable for only a short time.

AVOIDING INTERRUPTIONS

A cardinal rule of home office design is to keep the office and house as separate as possible. In reality this often is impossible. Working out a compromise—or at least an understanding—with others in the house will result in more productive work.

Studies show that a common place for shared office space is the bedroom or a room off the bedroom. This may be fine for teenagers or those who live alone. But if someone is sleeping nearby, how do you avoid interrupting his or her slumber as you rustle pages, tap on a keyboard, or activate a printer?

When assessing possible office locations, note traffic patterns in the home, then choose a location that is as out of the way as possible. It is almost impossible to get serious work done with people walking past your desk. The children—and everyone else in the house—need to know that the office space is where you work and you are not to be interrupted.

On the one hand, the office should be sited so that when you are on the phone, a client doesn't hear your pet bird chirping or baby crying in the background. On the other hand, you may not want to be too far removed from the action, particularly if you are a parent, because you could be distracted trying to figure out why doors are slamming or dishes are falling on the floor.

PUBLIC ACCESS

If clients visit your office, you need to take extra measures to present a professional appearance.

If your office happens to be in an enclosed porch, no other part of the house will be visible between the door and your work space. But if your office is in a converted upstairs room, visitors must travel through the house, possibly past unwashed dishes, unmade beds, and unswept floors.

If doable, keep the office on the first floor at the front of the house. If the area you select lacks a private entrance, remember that it is not particularly difficult to install a new door and walkway.

A professional appearance extends to bathrooms. If you have frequent visitors, designate a bathroom for their use. Keep it clean; remove personal items, such as prescriptions, from view; and make sure there are enough towels and toilet paper.

Clients and visitors should have a place to hang coats and set umbrellas. If they have to wait, provide comfortable seating with some reading material and perhaps some pleasant music.

Have tables, desks, and chairs to accommodate the maximum number of visitors you are likely to have at one time. An inexpensive folding table and chairs come in handy if you only occasionally receive several visitors; these items can be folded up and put into storage when no longer needed.

FIRST IMPRESSION: THE ENTRANCE

The entrance to your office is likely the first image clients have of you and your business. Think of the entrance as a part of your public face. Many business entrances include a sign. An attractive and professional looking entrance is important in turning that all-important first impression in your favor.

Make it easy for people to find you. If clients have trouble locating your house due to the lack of signs or a clearly visible address, they may become frustrated. If they are uncertain which door to enter, their doubts and discomfort increase. If, however, clients have no trouble finding your house or a place to park and they see an attractive entrance, they are likely to feel more comfortable with you and your services.

Keep walkways clear of snow, toys, and debris. Don't force visitors to confront your dog. Make sure stairs and railings are in good condition. Keep the lawn, shrubs, and flowers trimmed and healthy looking.

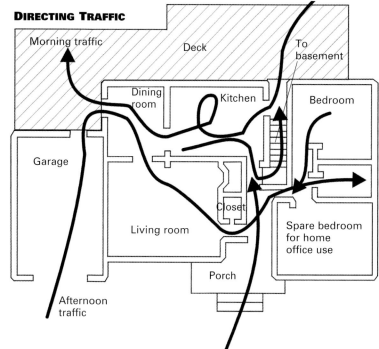

DIRECTING TRAFFIC

Morning traffic — Deck — To basement — Dining room — Kitchen — Bedroom — Garage — Closet — Living room — Spare bedroom for home office use — Porch — Afternoon traffic

Make sure that the entryway is well lighted. If visitors are likely to wait for the door to be answered, the entrance should be covered to protect them from rain and snow.

A flagstone walkway clearly defines the entry to this office over a garage.

PUBLIC ACCESS
continued

And remember that the costs of maintaining and cleaning your home office—and an entrance to it—may be tax deductible. (Check with an accountant or tax advisor before claiming the deduction.)

LANDSCAPING: DO YOUR GROUNDWORK

Successful landscape design complements the style and location of your house. If clients come to your home office, you can use landscaping to separate the business from the domestic affairs.

Handsome, tasteful landscaping reflects well on you and your business. There are many books and magazines on all aspects of landscaping. Landscape designers, including landscape architects, and landscape contractors can help you design and bring to life an attractive, functional, inviting entrance.

Use walkways and plantings to direct foot traffic toward the proper entrance. Fences can be used to keep visitors away from parts of the house you want off limits. High bushes and trees can hide family areas of the yard.

New windows and French doors help transform an old garage into a light, airy office just steps from the house.

OFFICE ORGANIZATION: KEEP IT CLEAN

A messy office may have a more personal, less institutional feel about it, but clients may not react that way. A clean, well-organized, comfortable office is a sign of professionalism.

If your work keeps you busy and clients visit regularly, consider hiring someone to do the cleaning. Paper clutter and disorganized office supplies can be cured with additional shelving and file cabinets. Spending a few minutes at the end of every work day putting files away and cleaning your desk can help.

INSURANCE: PLAY IT SAFE

You are responsible for the safety of visiting clients. Common sense suggests that you make sure your walkway has no uneven sections on which someone could trip and that the entryway is well lit. Talk with your insurance agent to be sure you have adequate liability coverage. Also keep in mind that the standard homeowner's policy may not cover home office equipment.

Outside the office above, an exuberant bougainvillea shades a patio that often serves as an informal conference area.

DESIGNING FOR ACCESSIBILITY

Even though the law may not require it, think about a barrier-free entrance to your home if you expect to be visited by handicapped or elderly clients. A barrier-free entrance and office allow more people to approach, enter, and use your home office.

Many people associate accessibility with the wheelchair ramps often tacked onto public buildings. But ramps are only one component of an accessible building, and they don't have to be ugly. In fact, many people prefer ramps to stairs. And everyone benefits from being able to wheel large loads into the house or office without confronting stairs.

An accessible entrance has a wide, smooth pathway to the door, is covered and lit, and has a functioning doorbell and a place to sit. A window offers visibility to visitors and occupants alike.

THE ENTRANCE

An accessible entrance should be free of stairs. The entryway or ramp leading to the door should slope gradually to make wheelchair use and walking safe and comfortable. The pathway from the parking area to the door should be concrete, asphalt, or other solid surface. Gravel is difficult to negotiate in a wheelchair.

If your driveway runs to a garage located under the house, consider installing a driveway on the other side that ends at the same level as the house or office entrance.

Pathways to the door should be wide— 5 feet is ideal. The surface should be smooth and continuous, with no threshold more than ½ inch high.

Place the entrance under an overhang, with seating nearby. Have lights at the door and along the pathway.

INDOORS

Doorways should have a clear opening of at least 32 inches, although 36 inches is better because it is easier to pass through in a wheelchair (and it is more convenient for moving large objects in and out of the office).

Wood or linoleum floors are easier to negotiate (and more durable) than carpeting. Doors with lever handles are easier to open for many people than those with knobs that must be twisted. The bathroom should have grab bars around the toilet and an open space under the sink to accommodate wheelchair users.

Steep stairs make it hard, or even impossible, for some to reach your office. Try to provide a step-free entrance.

Old driveway

New driveway

PLANNING FOR GROWTH

If you plan to run a business out of your home, you probably hope it will grow. One of the biggest mistakes you can make is constructing a home office unable to accommodate growth. Two of the most important considerations are planning for more employees and more files.

MAKING ROOM FOR EMPLOYEES

It's one thing to create an office that can handle occasional visitors or clients; it's another to have a regular employee, such as a part-time bookkeeper or full-time assistant. Hiring people to work in your home office involves legal, financial, and tax issues you should take up with appropriate professionals. From the standpoint of office design, however, you will have to provide room for an additional desk or work station and separate files. You also may need another phone line and additional parking.

SETTING RECORDS

Planning for growth means planning for the storage of records and files. Business records should be kept only as long as they serve a useful purpose or meet legal requirements. The American Institute of Certified Public Accountants has issued these guidelines on how long business records should be kept.
■ TAX RECORDS: Three years in current filing system, seven years in storage (the IRS destroys returns after seven years).
■ BANKING RECORDS, STATEMENTS, AND DEPOSIT SLIPS: Three years in current filing system, seven years in storage.
■ CANCELLED CHECKS AND INVOICES FOR THE PURCHASE OF ASSETS WHERE THE DETERMINATION OF TAX BASIS MAY BE IMPORTANT: Keep indefinitely.
■ PAYROLL RECORDS, W2 FORMS, 941 FORMS: Keep indefinitely.
■ PARTNERSHIP AND CORPORATION LICENSES, STOCK LEDGERS, BYLAWS, MINUTES: Keep indefinitely.
■ LEGAL CORRESPONDENCE, INCLUDING THAT PERTAINING TO COPYRIGHTS, BILLS OF SALE, AND PERMITS: Keep indefinitely.
■ INSURANCE DOCUMENTS: Three years in current filing system, seven years in storage.
■ PROPERTY RECORDS, APPRAISALS, BLUEPRINTS: Keep indefinitely.
■ PERSONNEL RECORDS: Seven years after termination of employment.
■ LEASES AND CONTRACTS: 10 years after termination.

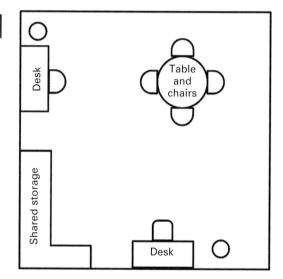

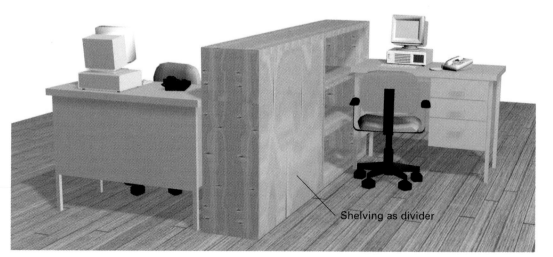

An office for two presents extra challenges. A compact arrangement uses shelves to divide separate desks. If space permits the desks to be separated, shared storage units and a table and chairs allow for meetings and discussion.

SETTING UP WORK STATIONS

An office provides an environment in which to work. Within the office, individual work stations serve as hubs for specific tasks. The most elemental office—a desk—is a single work station that can adapt to many uses. But a home office for a lone worker may involve multiple work stations if the work is diverse. For example, a home office for a photographer might have five distinct work stations:

■ A clear conference table.
■ A desk for computer and paperwork.
■ A table for sorting and filing.
■ A studio for photography.
■ A darkroom for processing.

Only you know your specific needs. As your business grows, you may need additional stations or additional people to handle the duties at specific work stations.

WORK SURFACES

"Work surface" is a more encompassing term than "desk." Generally speaking, a work surface should be 25–30 inches deep. The return—the short leg of an L-shape desk— is narrower, about 15 inches deep.

The nature of your work dictates the type of surface you need. Some people require only a small desk for paperwork, relying on a different surface for their major work. A plumber may need a surface that is more of a workbench than a traditional desk, and an architect needs a sturdy drafting table.

A FLEXIBLE WORKSTATION

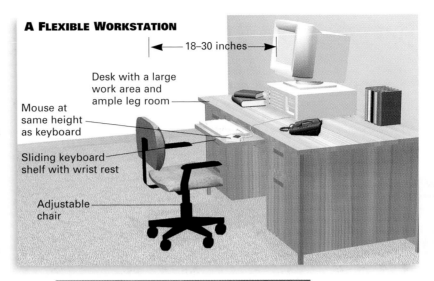

18–30 inches

Desk with a large work area and ample leg room

Mouse at same height as keyboard

Sliding keyboard shelf with wrist rest

Adjustable chair

FURNITURE

Take the time to peruse all price levels— the high-end office furniture stores, the discount chains, and used-furniture shops. You need to see what is available, even if it exceeds your budget, so you can judge and compare. Be forewarned—a sticker on a piece of furniture that says it is "ergonomically designed" doesn't mean it's comfortable.

Economizing is not always wise, however. Don't accept poor design. Besides fitting you, furniture should be adaptable to various work applications. It also should be compatible with other furniture designs.

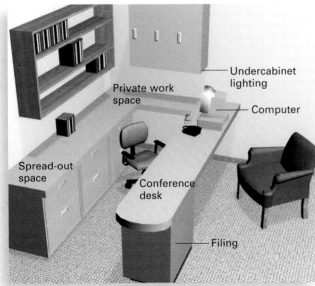

This U-shape work station serves multiple needs in a very efficient and compact space.

Undercabinet lighting

Private work space

Computer

Spread-out space

Conference desk

Filing

CHOOSING A CHAIR

For many, a chair is the most important furnishing in the home office. A well-designed chair can make your workday more productive and comfortable by preventing back and neck aches and reducing fatigue. A good office chair can cost several hundred dollars, but if you spend a significant amount of time sitting in your office, it is money well spent.

Modern office chairs are marvels of engineering. They include numerous adjustable features that allow you to tailor your chair to your body. Heavily padded chairs may seem the most comfortable, but the best designs offer:

■ A curved front edge of the seat, which limits pressure on the backs of your thighs.
■ Padded, adjustable arm rests.
■ A back that can be adjusted up and down as well as in and out.
■ A seat you can raise and lower quickly.
■ A five-wheel swivel base.

PREPARING A FLOOR PLAN

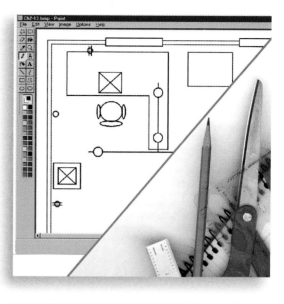

After you know what furniture you want but before you actually purchase it, draw a floor plan. This is easier than moving furnishings in and out to determine which pieces and configurations work.

A floor plan is a flat, two-dimensional diagram of space. To be useful it must be drawn accurately, showing the exact proportions and location of structural elements, such as walls, windows, closets, and doors, as well as radiators, electrical outlets, and phone jacks.

Floor plans are drawn to scale so the elements of the room represented on paper have the same relative size as the actual elements. For convenience, plans for a whole house are typically drawn to a scale in which ¼ inch represents 1 foot, but single rooms can be drawn at ½ inch or larger scale.

As you work on your plan, consider your storage needs. Well-planned storage makes an office efficient and attractive. If you fail to account for storage in your plan, you may find yourself outgrowing your office quickly.

Compact computer work stations provide a handy and affordable means of consolidating office equipment in a small area.

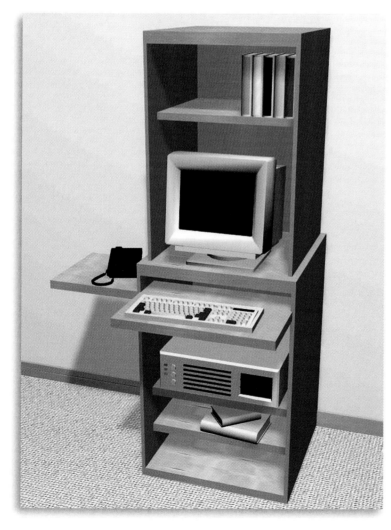

PLANNING FOR STORAGE

The keys to an efficient, uncluttered office are organization and storage, which go hand in hand. They are as important as having the correct desk and chair. Plan for two main categories of items:

■ MATERIALS AND EQUIPMENT, which you need to perform your work.

■ RECORDS AND RESEARCH amassed in producing and selling the work.

Most paperwork should be stored in file cabinets, where it will stay in good condition and be easy to retrieve. Materials, equipment, and other important items can be stored in an existing closet stripped of its poles and racks. Make shelves using inexpensive wire rack systems or utility-grade shelving.

If the room has no closet but is large enough, you can build one. If the room is too small, you can create storage elsewhere in the home, keeping only the most-used items near or in your workspace.

Before launching into storage solutions, decide what to store. Some people are pack rats and keep everything. In an office, piles of paper, stacks of books, and assorted miscellany look unprofessional and hinder efficiency.

SORTING AND DISCARDING

You need to make a conscious, constant effort to fight clutter. Walking into an office stacked with papers can have a depressing effect because the clutter looks like unfinished work. You also waste valuable time looking for things. Discarding or filing all that paper will make you look more professional and inspire you to sit down and start working.

DRAWING THE PLAN

To start, make a rough sketch of the floor plan. Indicate positions of permanent features, such as doors, windows, electrical outlets, phone and cable TV jacks, and heat registers, even if they are not at floor level. Mark the direction of the swing of any doors and casement windows.

Now add measurements to the sketch. Using a tape measure, work your way around the perimeter of the room, preferably at floor level, where it's easier to get an accurate reading, measuring all walls and wall segments, including jogs. As you take each measurement, jot it on the sketch. Go back and measure the length and width of the room, wall to wall. Check that wall segments add up to the total wall dimension. Note the width of window and door openings and their frames, and measure the arc of the door swing. Mark any features that protrude into the room, such as wall cabinets or fireplace mantels.

Next, make a correctly scaled drawing of the plan. Purchase a pad of graph paper or, if you want a larger scale to work with, make your own grid. Carefully transfer all the information from your rough sketch to the grid with pencil and ruler, using an adjustable triangle to help get angles and corners right. When you have everything in place, finish the drawing with a narrow-tipped felt pen. (To avoid smearing the ink, tape pennies to the underside of the ruler, and hold the pen barrel against its edge.)

ROOM FOR A COMPUTER

Most home offices now revolve around the computer with its monitor, keyboard, mouse, speakers, printer, scanner, and modem. Making space for such an array of equipment, as well as fax machines, copiers, phones, and other machines, is an important part of a well-designed floor plan.

Include measurements of the equipment you have—or expect to get—and include them in your planning. Consider whether you need to keep all of the equipment close together, and whether you prefer it be grouped vertically or horizontally. A vertical approach uses more wall space and less floor space by stacking components. Some people feel overwhelmed by having so much electronic gear so close. Moreover, a printer placed above you may be hard to fix in the event of a paper jam. Stacked configurations may not accommodate a larger computer setup if you decide to upgrade.

Often it is better to spread computer equipment over several pieces of furniture than crowd it onto one, even though it consumes more floor space. The keyboard and mouse should fit on a convenient platform, such as an adjustable keyboard drawer that slides under the desk.

KEY TO SYMBOLS

○
Phone jack

Electrical outlet

Overhead light

$
Switch

Window

Door

Bifold door

If you're looking at an architect's building plans, or if you want a contractor to understand yours, these standard symbols will help.

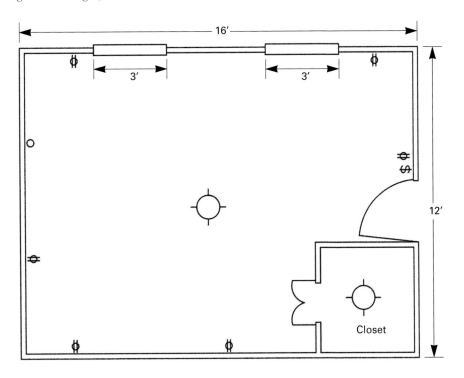

ARRANGING THE ELEMENTS

With the preliminary floor plan drawn, the next step is to make some decisions about office furnishings and equipment. What will you keep, what will you discard, what will you add, and where will you put it?

A COMPLETE FLOOR PLAN

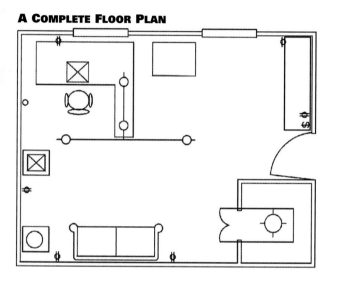

As you consider how you might arrange the space, furnishings, and equipment, keep a few important points in mind. The plan should revolve around the primary function of the room and the features that support it.

Once again, planning on paper is the most efficient way to proceed. Scaled furniture templates are available in art-supply stores or you make miniature cutouts of the pieces of furniture, with their width and length accurately drawn to the same scale as your floor plan.

BASIC LAYOUTS

As you work on your layout, you'll discover that there are fewer choices than you thought. You also will realize there is no perfect layout.

There are two major areas of concern: the room and what goes in it. The principle room components are the walls, windows, and door—the room's structural features. Sub-categories include the size of the room, the color of the walls, and the amount and kind of light entering the space. What goes in the room involves the desk, chairs, file cabinets, floor lamps, tables, and other equipment.

It is best to begin your layout with the basics: the work surface and chair. Once the location of these is decided, the placement of other components, such as file cabinets, bookcases, and lamps, is logical. For example, the printer and fax machine should be within easy reach of the desk chair.

THE FINAL LAYOUT

Position the larger pieces of furniture first, then the smaller items. Move the shapes around until you find an arrangement you like. Carefully lay a piece of tracing paper on top of your plan and trace the outlines of the room and furnishings. To be certain you have left enough space to open file drawers and doors, use a dotted line to indicate the area

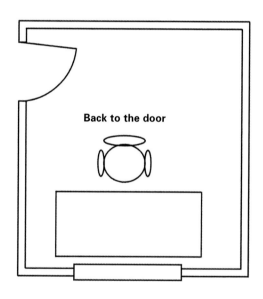

Back to the door

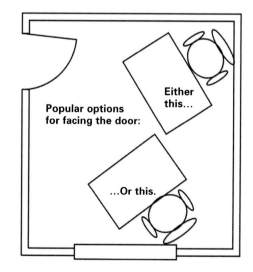

Popular options for facing the door:

Either this...

...Or this.

that the opened items will occupy. Also, be sure you have allowed enough space around and among furnishings for people to walk, sit comfortably, and reach forward. As you consider your various office furniture plans, evaluate each in light of the intended functions of the room and your work patterns.

When you have settled on a plan you like, make several copies.

EVALUATING THE WIRING

Some unharried home workers can retire to a small shed out back with a pencil and paper or manual typewriter and function perfectly. Most of us, however, must be wired extensively to run the machines that keep our businesses. If you plan to put your office in an existing space, show all electrical switches, outlets, and phone jacks on your final layout. Running new wiring can be time-consuming and expensive, so try to utilize as much of the existing wiring as possible.

While you are at it, check that your electrical service has been upgraded to serve today's needs. Outlets should accept three-pronged plugs and be properly grounded. (In fact, you may void the warranty on some computer and surge protection equipment by plugging it into ungrounded circuits.) To check for proper grounding, buy a plug-in circuit analyzer. These handy, inexpensive devices have three small lights. When plugged in, you compare the pattern of lights with the code printed on the analyzer. If there is a problem with the wiring, you will know immediately.

A related issue has come to be known as "wire management," which is just a fancy name for the process of keeping the spaghetti of computer cords off the floor. It's a significant aesthetic and safety issue. Wire management may include channels along the backs of work surfaces, pockets for surge suppressors, cutouts for wire runs, and even hollow furniture legs.

FURNITURE TEMPLATES

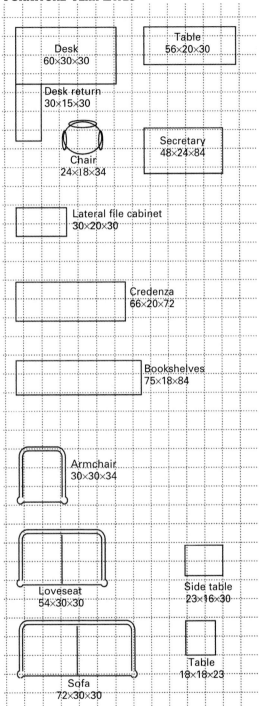

Desk
60×30×30

Table
56×20×30

Desk return
30×15×30

Chair
24×18×34

Secretary
48×24×84

Lateral file cabinet
30×20×30

Credenza
66×20×72

Bookshelves
75×18×84

Armchair
30×30×34

Loveseat
54×30×30

Side table
23×16×30

Sofa
72×30×30

Table
18×18×23

BRIGHT IDEAS

Once you have an idea of how the office will be arranged, consider the room's lighting. It pays to know what you need before you shop. Fixtures are expensive, and although you might be able to return a floor lamp, any more permanent fixture you install likely will be yours for keeps.

Your first concerns should be assessing what you want the lighting to accomplish, where you need it, and how much you can spend. Also, take into account the room's natural light.

LIGHT SOURCES

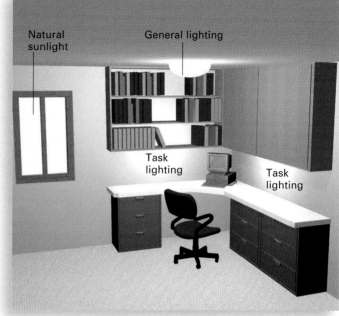

Natural sunlight · General lighting · Task lighting · Task lighting

NATURAL LIGHT

Natural light brightens a home office and produces positive psychological effects. Diffused natural light, such as that in a north-facing room, is best because it is easy on the eyes. The intense glare of the afternoon sun in a west-facing office may necessitate window shades, as well as additional cooling.

If you are working with your back to a window, glare on your computer screen can be a problem. Experts suggest locating your computer so you are facing a window, as long as the sun does not hit the computer, overheating it. This enables you to look up from the screen and out the window, relieving eyestrain. Direct sunshine may present a harsh contrast, however, so use blinds, shades, or other window treatments to regulate the amount of light.

A basement office may not get much natural light. The best sources are windows that face south or southwest. To maximize light, clear away any obstructions in front of basement windows.

If you need more natural light in an attic office, consider installing a skylight. If possible, have it face north to provide diffuse light.

ELECTRICAL LIGHT

Comfortable, practical, and pleasing office light is usually produced through a combination of three types of electrical illumination: general, task, and accent lighting. How much you use of each depends on personal preference and room layout.

KEEPING SUNLIGHT IN SIGHT OR OVER YOUR SHOULDER

Facing a sunny window can have you squinting at your computer screen; a bright window behind you can cast stark shadows on your work. You might prefer the position illustrated above. Visit offices to determine your preference before cutting holes in walls.

GENERAL LIGHTING. Also known as background or ambient lighting, general lighting provides a low to moderate level of illumination for a particular area or room, sufficient to see people and objects clearly but not uncomfortably bright. General lighting works best when a number of light sources, such as ceiling and wall fixtures, are used together.

TASK LIGHTING. Task, or localized, lighting provides adequate, suitable light for specific activities, such as reading or drafting. Whether the fixture is suspended, sitting on a table, or directed downward from the ceiling, it is intended to illuminate the work surface or the task at hand.

ACCENT LIGHTING. This type of lighting, also called decorative lighting, draws the eye to objects or areas that merit special attention—a display on a shelf, a painting, an exotic plant. Sometimes accent lighting is used to create a particular mood.

ADDING LIGHT TO THE PLAN

Once you have considered how the room should be lit, start adding your lighting scheme to the final floor plan.

Begin with general lighting. Sketch in the areas where you would like to see light focus or flow across walls or fill a corner. Think about how you'd get the light to those areas and indicate it on your plan.

Next, locate all the areas on the plan where task lighting will be required. Sketch in the fixtures you have in mind, including lamps you intend to reuse that already are not

TRACK LIGHTING

One of the most versatile lighting systems, track lighting can be indispensable when decorating or redecorating. It can be mounted on almost any ceiling or wall, regardless of the material, and arranged in almost any configuration. The individual fixtures come in a number of sizes and finishes and often accept a variety of bulbs. A track system can solve all the lighting needs of a room. Some fixtures work together to flood walls with uniform light for general illumination, others can be directed to assist specific tasks, and still others can highlight decorative accents. Another advantage is that, if you move, the system can be dismantled and set up in a new space.

on the furniture plan. Finally, indicate accent lighting you hope to incorporate.

When the time comes to select the actual lighting for your design, you may have to make some compromises. If your budget doesn't allow the purchase of a track system and new table and floor lamps, for instance, it may be wiser to invest in track lighting and find inexpensive lamps. You can always replace the interim lamps later.

SERVICE PANEL

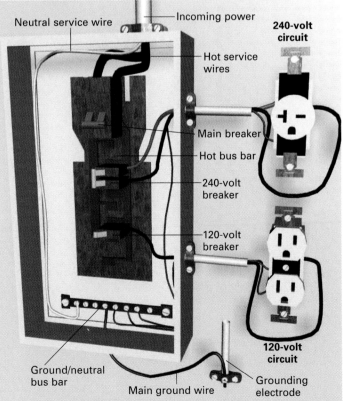

INSTALLING TRACK LIGHTING

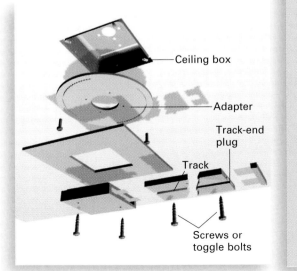

This built-in storage wall holds one family's electronic needs, including a compact office with a file cabinet. Made from maple veneer plywood, the unit spans 15 feet and stands 9 feet tall.

BUILDING SKILLS

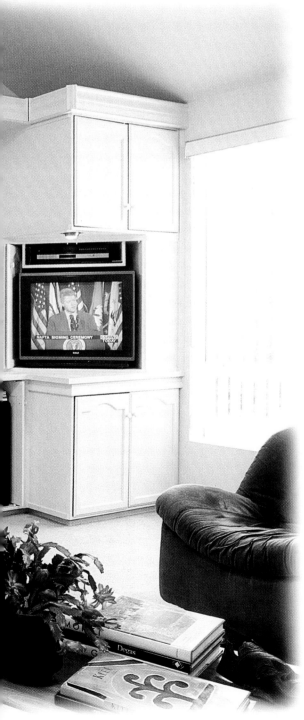

Creating a home office is rarely as simple as buying furniture and moving it into a vacant space. Usually, you have to make at least a few modifications. These range from installing phones and painting to building walls and adding windows. Most of these tasks are easier than they might seem, and many can be accomplished by a determined homeowner.

   Whether you plan to do the work yourself or hire it out, this chapter offers essential step-by-step information that helps you get the job done right.

   Thorough planning keeps headaches to a minimum. Planning includes rounding up all the necessary tools and materials and enlisting helpers. Then it's up to you to stay focused, and follow each step correctly.

   Often, what distinguishes the work of a professional from that of a do-it-yourselfer is not quality but the amount of time it takes to complete the job. Give yourself enough time to ensure quality.

Wall Framing Basics

Partition walls, which divide space inside a building, are classified as bearing walls, which support the house, or non-bearing walls, which support only themselves.

BEARING WALLS

The exterior walls of a house are bearing walls. You can recognize interior bearing walls by looking in the attic and basement. If ceiling joists run perpendicular to the direction of the wall below, the wall is probably bearing, especially if the joists are overlapped or spliced. In the basement or crawl space, look for beams or doubled or tripled joists resting on footings. Walls directly above them are probably bearing. Removing and constructing bearing walls is a major structural alteration; if done incorrectly, it could weaken a house.

MATERIALS

Use 2×4s or 2×6s for the studs and plates, 4×6s or doubled 2×6s for door and window headers. The length of the studs will depend on the height of your ceilings.

Nails come in a variety of types and lengths, and are designated by the term "penny." For framing walls, use 16d common nails, which are 3½ inches long. For attaching top plates to ceilings, use 4-inch wood screws. Using a power screwdriver or electric drill with a Phillips-head bit, drive

the screws through the top plate and ceiling material into the joists or the blocking above it. This is much easier than nailing overhead and less likely to cause cracks in the ceiling.

BUILDING A WALL

There are several ways to build an interior partition wall in an existing room. Begin by stripping away the baseboard and wallcovering where the new wall will intersect the existing wall so you can nail the new wall to stud or horizontal blocking set in place.

If you are building more than one wall, construct the longest walls first. Start with the corner posts, which are doubled studs separated by scraps of 2×4 placed between the studs at the top, middle, and bottom.

Here are three methods for framing a wall to fit between an existing floor and ceiling.
■ Cut the top and bottom plates to length and stack them on the floor where the wall will be located. Then lay out the stud locations and measure between the stacked plates and the ceiling to determine the length of each stud. Cut the studs and nail them to the top plate. Tilt the frame up and slip the bottom plate beneath the studs. Attach the top plate to the ceiling and nail the bottom plate to the floor. Then toenail all the studs to the bottom plate, making sure each one is plumb.

CLUES FOR RECOGNIZING BEARING WALLS
FROM ABOVE...

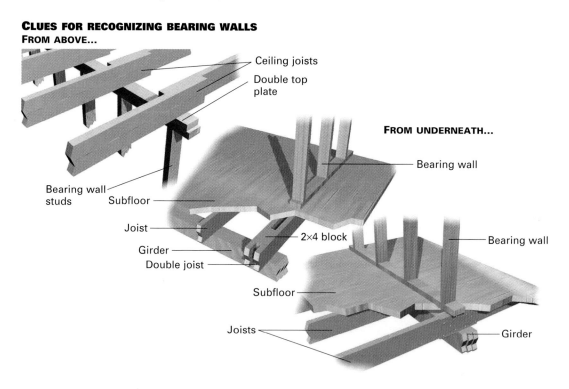

Ceiling joists

Double top plate

FROM UNDERNEATH...

Bearing wall

Bearing wall studs

Subfloor

Joist

Girder

Double joist

2×4 block

Bearing wall

Subfloor

Joists

Girder

■ Cut the studs ¼ inch short and assemble the entire wall on the floor. Then tilt it into place; the wall frame should clear the ceiling as you tilt it up. Fill the space between the top plate and ceiling with shims.

■ Nail the top and bottom plates in place. Then measure, cut, and toenail each stud into the plates. This method should be used if you do not have enough space to assemble the complete wall on the floor.

ATTACHING WALLS

If the new wall runs parallel to existing joists and is located between them, install 2×4 blocking between the joists. If you aren't removing the finished ceiling and don't have access from above, cut 3-inch-wide openings in the ceiling. Then insert the blocks and secure them with screws.

If the new wall is short or is intersected by another new wall that is nailed firmly into joists because it runs perpendicular to them, you can use toggle bolts to attach the new wall to the ceiling.

TWO WAYS TO FRAME A WALL

Joists

Cut openings

Install blocking

Drive nails or screws into joists

Corner assembly

Top plate

Marked bottom plate

Corner post

Bottom plate

Studs

JOINING WALLS

Top plate

Existing studs

New nailing blocks

New end stud

Bottom plate

New walls can be framed in place or assembled on the floor and raised into position. They must be anchored securely after you have them plumb and square with the rest of the room.

Fasten wall to joists or overhead blocking

SPECIAL FRAMING

A typical wall is framed with 2×4s spaced 16 inches *on center*, that is, the centers of the studs fall every 16 inches along the plates. When a door or window interrupts the framing, you must frame a rough opening. When you buy a door or window, the manufacturer should tell you the size of the rough opening needed. The most important part of a rough opening is the header, which is the horizontal member just above the door or window. The header must be big enough to transfer the load from that portion of the wall to the sides of the rough opening.

SIZING HEADERS

Headers are usually made out of solid beams such as 4×4s, 4×6s, or built up with 2×4s set on edge with a ½-inch plywood spacer in between. The size of the required header varies according to the type and grade of lumber and the size of the opening. As a rule of thumb, in a single-story building or on a top floor, the 4× or built-up 2× header should be as deep in nominal inches as the opening is wide in feet. Thus, in a 4-foot-wide rough opening, use a 4×4 or built-up 2×4 header. That same header should be used on the lower floor of a two-story house in a rough opening no wider than 3 feet. If you have questions about how big to make the header, consult a construction professional.

You can create privacy without building new walls. Bookcases, filing cabinets, or other storage units can separate one part of the room from another. Office supply stores also carry easy-to-assemble wall panels that do not require any carpentry.

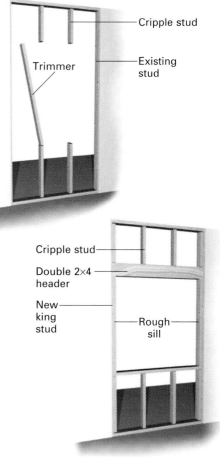

Cripple stud

Trimmer

Existing stud

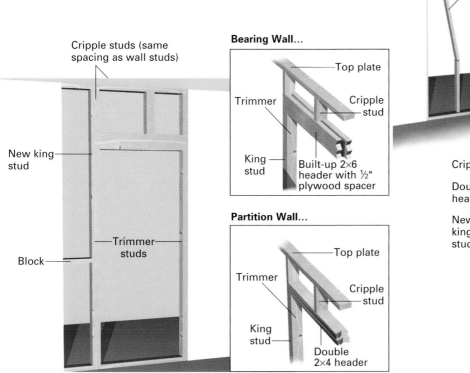

Cripple studs (same spacing as wall studs)

New king stud

Trimmer studs

Block

Bearing Wall...

Top plate

Trimmer

Cripple stud

King stud

Built-up 2×6 header with ½" plywood spacer

Partition Wall...

Top plate

Trimmer

Cripple stud

King stud

Double 2×4 header

Cripple stud

Double 2×4 header

New king stud

Rough sill

PLUMBING A HALF BATH

Installing a new half bathroom near your office does not necessarily require a lot of room or a large budget. But don't attempt to install drain and supply lines unless you have a good understanding of plumbing. Otherwise, hire a plumber to take care of this part of the project—the rough plumbing. Then you can install and hook up the fixtures yourself—the finish plumbing.

FINDING THE SPACE

Your local building code will probably specify the minimum space required around the toilet and sink. The sample floor plans at the right demonstrate how large a space you will likely need to create an acceptable bathroom. By using space-saving fixtures, you can shave a little more square footage where space is tight.

INSTALLING DRAIN LINES

The closer the new bathroom is to the house's main drain line or soil stack, the easier it will be to plumb. Center the toilet flange 12 inches from the finished wall, and screw it in place at the floor's finished height.

Run 3-inch plastic drainpipe from the flange to the soil stack. The pipe must slope downward from the flange at least ¼ inch per foot. Cut the pipe with a handsaw and join it with the cement recommended for the type of plastic you use either PVC or ABS. Support the drainpipe with hangers every 32 inches. Connect the 3-inch pipe to the 4-inch soil stack with a no-hub coupling.

Install a 1½-inch drain line for the sink. Run vent lines—2-inch-diameter for the toilet, 1½-inch for the sink—through the roof.

INSTALLING SUPPLY LINES

Water supply lines rely on pressure rather than gravity and are therefore easier to install. Cut into existing hot and cold water lines at a convenient location and run ½-inch copper pipes to the sink and toilet. Joining copper pipe requires a pipe cutter, propane torch, flux, and solder. Support the pipe with hangers every 6 feet. Place the supply valves on the wall at locations recommended by the fixture manufacturers.

If the bathroom is located in a remote part of your house, it may be more economical to install a tankless water heater, which can be mounted in a cabinet under the sink.

3×7-foot half bath with pocket door.

FINAL STEPS

Install electrical boxes for lights and switches, and a GFCI (ground-fault circuit interrupter) receptacle. Have the plumbing and wiring inspected, if necessary. Finish the wall and the floor. Install the toilet, sink, and door.

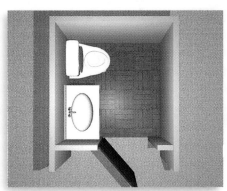

A 25-square-foot, 5×5-foot half bath.

COMMON PLUMBING TOOLS AND SUPPLIES

A bathroom adjacent to your home office can help meet your household needs before and after business hours. Just be sure it's always available and presentable for clients.

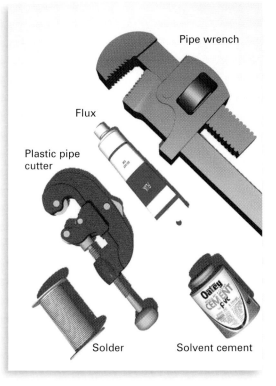

Pipe wrench

Flux

Plastic pipe cutter

Solder   Solvent cement

MEETING ELECTRICAL NEEDS

If your office's electrical outlets cannot provide enough power to run a computer, printer, copier, and other equipment, add a new circuit or extend an underused one. The best time to run wiring is when the walls are open.

DETERMINE THE LOAD

Begin by determining how much current the equipment in your office will draw. Isolate the outlets in the room by turning off the various breakers; stamped on the breaker switch is the maximum amps it will allow before tripping. Check to see what else is connected to the circuit in other rooms.

Then look for the wattages on the name plate of every appliance to be plugged into that circuit. Add up the wattages and divide by 120 (the voltage). If the number is close to or exceeds the breaker rating, add an additional circuit.

ADDING A CIRCUIT

For 15-amp circuits, use type NM 14-gauge two-wire cable with a bare or green ground wire. For a 20-amp circuit use cable with 12-gauge wire.

A tankless— "point-of-use"—water heater can supply hot water to a sink without having to run pipes from the main water heater.

To install cable where the wiring runs perpendicular to the framing, drill ¾-inch holes through the centers of the framing members. When running wire alongside a joist, staple it every 4½ feet.

For work in walls that aren't open, *fish* the wire through the bottom or top plates and into the walls, or mount surface *raceways* along the baseboard of the room. In the former situation, pull 6–8 inches of wire through a hole you've drilled in the wall, strip off the wire covering, and remove the insulation from the wire. Connect cable to metal or plastic outlet boxes using metal or plastic connectors. Attach the wires to the screw terminals of the new receptacle, or insert them into terminal holes in the back. Attach the white wire to the neutral terminal, which has nickel-plated screws; connect black wires to the side of the receptacle with brass screws. The ground wire is attached to the green screw marked "ground" on the outlet; if the electrical box is metal, the ground wire also should be attached to the box by means of a short wire, or pigtail. After attaching the wires, fold the wiring back into the box and screw the receptacle to the box. Attach a cover plate after painting is completed. A licensed electrician should connect the new circuit to the service panel.

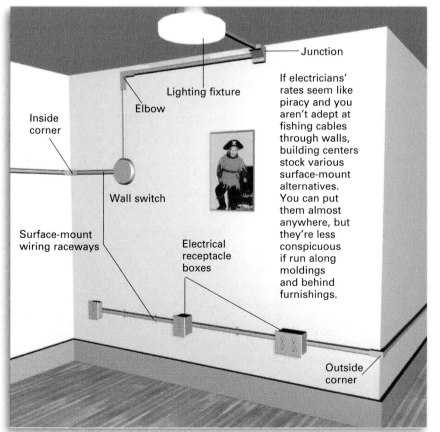

Junction

Lighting fixture

Elbow

Inside corner

Wall switch

Surface-mount wiring raceways

Electrical receptacle boxes

If electricians' rates seem like piracy and you aren't adept at fishing cables through walls, building centers stock various surface-mount alternatives. You can put them almost anywhere, but they're less conspicuous if run along moldings and behind furnishings.

Outside corner

Running cable in new construction

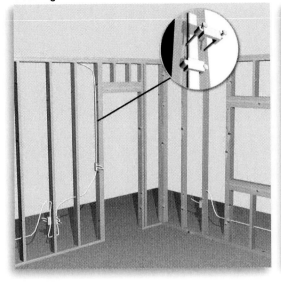

Running cable through existing walls

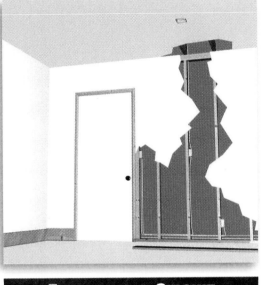

WIRING FOR COMMUNICATIONS

Today's home office communicates with the world through telephones, fax machines, and computer modems, each of which requires a telephone line. You can handle all these devices on a single line, but it's much more convenient to use two or three separate lines. Telephone companies now offer many services that help. A "voice mail" system, for example, allows you to receive messages while you are on the line with other business.

You own the telephone wiring and equipment in your home starting at the network interface, which is usually located in the basement or attic near the place where the phone cable enters your home. You can run new phone wiring from the interface. The low-voltage phone circuit cannot electrocute you, although you should lift off the handset to keep from being shocked if it rings.

From below, staple the wire to floor joists and pass it through a ¼-inch hole drilled in the floor. From above, you can fish the wire through the top plate and into a wall cavity. Feed the wire through a hole in the wall just above the baseboard.

Install more phone modules than you think you will need. That will allow you to expand or to move devices around the office.

EXTENDING A CIRCUIT

Find a junction box—often in the attic or basement—for the circuit to be extended. Install the new outlet boxes and run the wiring from them to the junction box. Wire receptacles into the new outlet boxes. Then turn off the power to the junction box and connect the new wiring to the circuit wiring inside it. First, remove the cover to the box and carefully pull all the wires straight out. Using a hammer and screwdriver, tap in one of the knockouts and twist it off. Attach the new cable to the box with a metal or plastic connector, leaving about 12 inches of cable protruding from the box. Strip the cable and wires.

To connect the new wires to the circuit wiring, unscrew the wire connectors from the old wires one at a time and connect the new wires to them—white to white, black to black, ground to ground. Twist the connectors back on or use new, larger connectors, if necessary. Gently push the wires back the way you found them, making sure all stripped wire is covered by connectors. Replace the cover, turn on the power, and test the new receptacles.

Fish cable through wall plates

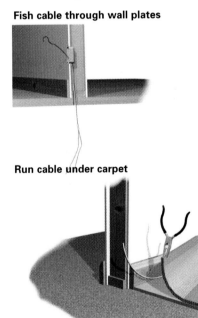

Run cable under carpet

Feed cable through wall

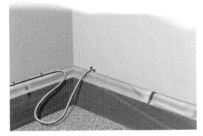

HEATING AND COOLING

If you plan to spend many hours a day in your home office, make it as comfortable as possible. Figuring out how to get heat and cool air to the office is critical to your comfort and can be one of the biggest and most expensive parts of the project.

EXPANDING AN OLD SYSTEM

If the office is in or connected to the house, you may be able to extend the existing thermal system. A good heating and cooling contractor can tell you if your system has the capacity to serve the new space.

FORCED AIR SYSTEMS require new ducts, which take a lot of room. You may be able to boost the delivery capacity of heated or cooled air by adding a more powerful fan.

HOT WATER SYSTEMS generally require less space when extended because they rely on small pipes, not large ducts, to deliver heat. However, you will need to make room for radiators or baseboard convectors. Another circulating pump can be added to push the additional water through the new piping loop.

ADDING A NEW SYSTEM

If your office is in a separate structure, or if your house system can't serve additional space, you will have to install a new system.

AIR CONDITIONING can be supplied by a window unit. Most room-sized models operate on standard household current, so installation is relatively easy.

ELECTRICAL HEATERS are inexpensive to buy but costly to operate. They are a good choice for an office that rarely needs heat.

DIRECT-VENT GAS HEATERS operate on natural gas or propane (LP gas). They are vented through the wall, and do not require a flue. Wall-mounted models take little space and are least expensive. Attractive new units resemble wood stoves or fireplaces.

WOOD, COAL, AND PELLET STOVES are excellent sources of heat, but require expensive flues and must be fed fuel and cleaned regularly.

ADDING A NEW SYSTEM

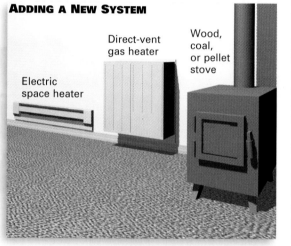

Electric space heater

Direct-vent gas heater

Wood, coal, or pellet stove

EXTENDING THE EXISTING SYSTEM

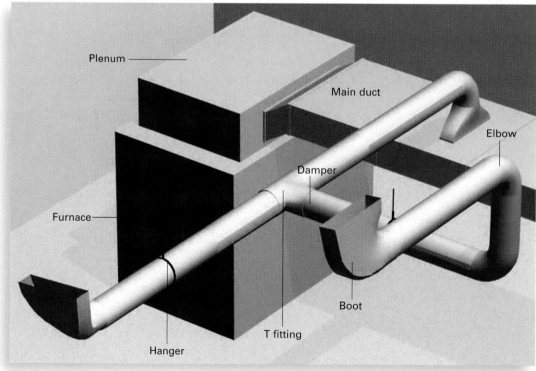

Plenum

Main duct

Elbow

Damper

Furnace

Boot

T fitting

Hanger

SOUNDPROOFING

Most people prefer to work in as quiet a setting as possible, and other members of the household would probably prefer not to have their activities disrupted by noises emanating from your home office. The best way to minimize noise is to set up the office in a remote part of the house or in a separate structure. Since that is not always possible, here are some techniques for reducing the transmission of sound in the house.

UNDERSTANDING SOUND

Sound waves pass through air, creating vibrations that bounce around rooms and are transmitted through walls, ceilings, and floors. By adding materials that absorb sound waves, you reduce noise. The performance of sound-absorbing materials depends on thickness, porosity, and resistance to air flow.

IF THESE WALLS COULD TALK

Sound transmission, especially of high-frequency sounds, can be simply cut by adding mass to the wall, such as an additional layer of wallboard. (If possible, install the new drywall to sound channels placed on the existing layer. Use ⅝-inch rather than ½-inch drywall for added sound absorption.

An even wider range of frequencies can be absorbed by adding fiberglass insulation in the wall. The most effective wall of this type utilizes offset studs (*shown at right*). The studs are attached to 4-inch-wide plates on 8-inch centers and are staggered with a ½-inch offset. Wall cavities are filled with fiberglass batts and covered with ½-inch drywall.

Acoustical plaster and other sound-reducing compounds can be applied to drywall surfaces.

MUFFLING VOICES FROM ABOVE

Floors and ceilings can benefit from some of the same treatments recommended for walls, including, adding mass and fiberglass. Offsetting floor or ceiling joists is not practical, however. Instead, vibration reducing sound channels can be added on the bottom of the joists, separating the drywall from the framing. It also helps to sheathe the floor with a double layer of plywood or a layer each of plywood and particleboard, then add thick padding and thick carpet.

KEEP IT DOWN

You can reduce the transmission of sound waves within a room by using sound-absorbing materials to deaden vibration. This approach is most effective if followed in the room where the noise is being made. Install thick carpeting over a thick pad. Install acoustical panels on the ceiling, suspended in aluminum frames, but do not paint the panels, since that would dramatically reduce their sound-absorbing capacity. Hang heavy curtains or drapes on the windows and weatherstrip around the door. Replace hollow-core doors with a solid wood or insulated doors.

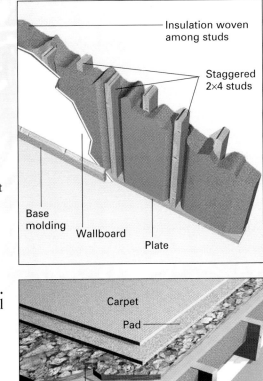

Insulation woven among studs

Staggered 2×4 studs

Base molding

Wallboard

Plate

Carpet

Pad

Particleboard

Plywood

Fiberglass batts

Sound channel

Joists

Drywall

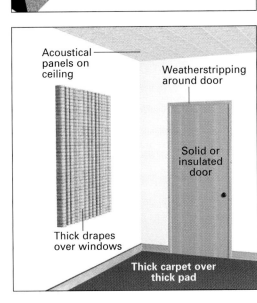

Acoustical panels on ceiling

Weatherstripping around door

Solid or insulated door

Thick drapes over windows

Thick carpet over thick pad

INSTALLING WALLBOARD

Before covering walls and ceilings, be sure all framing, wiring, plumbing, and insulation have been roughed in and inspected. Drywall panels are 4 feet wide and come in 8- and 12-foot lengths. For ease of handling, use 4×8 sheets, ½- or ⅝-inch thick, unless the ceilings are higher than 8 feet or you plan to hang the panels with their long dimension parallel to the floor. The fewer the joints, the better.

If installing drywall panels horizontally, start from the top of the wall and work down. You can cover gaps at the bottom with narrow pieces of drywall, which will be hidden behind the baseboard.

CUTTING PANELS

Lay the drywall on a flat surface and use a straightedge to guide your utility knife. Score the drywall on one side. Then tilt the sheet upright and, pushing with your knee against the side opposite of the cut, fold the drywall far enough to snap the hard inner core. Use the utility knife to finish the cut on the back side of the drywall.

Use a keyhole saw to cut openings for outlets and switches. Place the drywall against the wall, making sure that the opening is over the outlet or switch.

Don't bother making advance cutouts for doors or windows. Just cut the overhang with a handsaw after the drywall has been fastened to the studs.

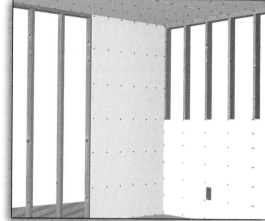

Stagger the joints

Score with utility knife and straightedge

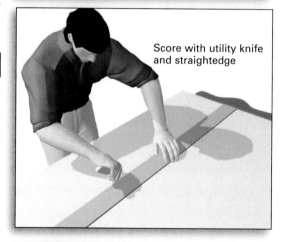

Snap

Drive screws into framing

FASTENING WALLBOARD

Joints between drywall panels should fall atop studs. If they don't, add lumber nailers to the framing where drywall panels will meet.

Fasten the panels with drywall screws 12 inches apart and at least ⅜ inch in from the edge of the panel. Drive the screws deep enough into the paper surface for the joint compound to cover them. Avoid breaking through the paper; if that happens, install another screw nearby.

FINISHING WALLS AND CEILINGS

Offices are traditionally painted white or in institutional shades of gray or beige. With your home office, you have more freedom to use colors and coverings to create a personal zone of comfort and creativity. Choose colors that create the emotional atmosphere you desire, and use different shades to lighten or darken a room.

If clients will visit, try not to be too dramatic or eccentric with colors and patterns. The more public the space will be, the more you should emphasize neutral, light colors. A few colorful pieces of art may be all you need to add life to the room.

FINISHING WALLBOARD

Your goal is to create a smooth surface over all seams and nail heads. For taping and filling joints, you'll need 4-inch, 6-inch, and 12-inch putty knives and a "mud" tray used specifically for finish work. To complete the job, you'll need a long-handled drywall sander.

Although you can mix your own joint compound for small repairs, pre-mixed compound is best for new drywall construction. Sanding between coats makes a lot of dust. Wear goggles and a respirator. Seal passages to other rooms to contain the dust.

Spread compound over joint

Embed joint tape in compound and cover with thin layer of compound. Sand when dry.

PAINT AND PAPER

When you have a smooth finish, you are ready to prime and paint the drywall or cover it with wallpaper. Prime the new drywall before painting. Acrylic latex primers have little odor and clean up easily with soap and water. You can apply a latex or alkyd (oil-based) paint over the latex primer.

If you decide to hang wallpaper, smooth out any uneven surfaces and prime the walls with a product specifically formulated for use under wallpaper.

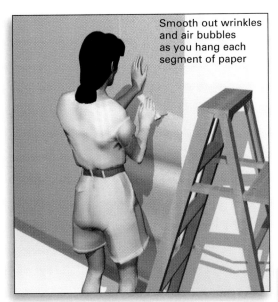

Smooth out wrinkles and air bubbles as you hang each segment of paper

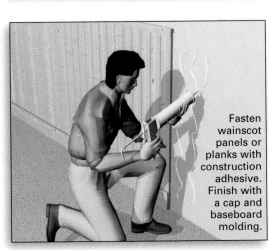

Fasten wainscot panels or planks with construction adhesive. Finish with a cap and baseboard molding.

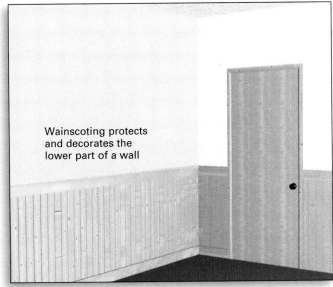

Wainscoting protects and decorates the lower part of a wall

FINISHING THE FLOOR

The floor covering you select for your home office should be an integral part of the overall design scheme. Popular options include carpet, wood, tile, and vinyl. Each has benefits and drawbacks, and your choice may reflect a compromise between comfort and durability or cost and ease of maintenance. An office with heavy foot traffic should have a floor that can withstand it. Chairs and other rolling equipment work best on a hard, smooth floor, but noise abatement and comfort may sway you toward carpet. Another factor to consider is that some flooring types can be installed quickly and inexpensively while others keep the room out of service for days or weeks.

Newer laminate flooring products are gaining acceptance and may be suitable for an office that needs a durable floor. Laminate floors are similar to plastic laminates used on kitchen countertops. The plastic coating is highly resistant to scratches. Laminate floors are easy to clean and relatively easy to install. The edges of the planks are glued together, allowing the floor to "float" on top of the subfloor. Laminate floors are prefinished, but they cannot be repaired easily and should not be used in wet areas.

Where there is an existing floor, its type may affect your choice of covering. In rooms with concrete floors, vinyl or ceramic tile often can be installed right over the concrete. Wood-frame floors may require an additional layer or two of plywood.

INSTALL IT YOURSELF?

CARPET
Can be installed quickly and inexpensively by a professional. Requires special tools to accurately measure, cut, and seam.

WOOD
Time consuming and messy, but manageable for a do-it-yourselfer with basic woodworking skills. Special installation and sanding tools can be rented from the dealer or a rental outlet.

TILE
Can be quite time-consuming if the floor is not level and solid. Requires accurate layout and careful attention to detail. Special tools usually can be borrowed or rented from the tile dealer.

VINYL
Vinyl tiles can be installed easily and quickly. Larger sheets require accurate measurement and cutting. Professional installation is often inexpensive and may be included in the cost of the material.

ANATOMY OF A WOOD FRAME FLOOR

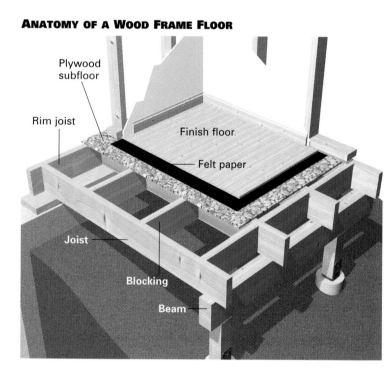

- Plywood subfloor
- Rim joist
- Finish floor
- Felt paper
- Joist
- Blocking
- Beam

ANATOMY OF A CONCRETE SLAB FLOOR

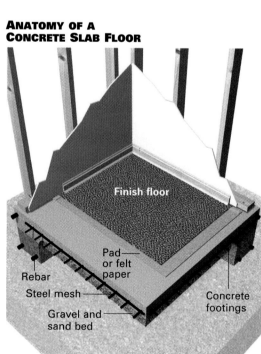

- Finish floor
- Pad or felt paper
- Rebar
- Steel mesh
- Gravel and sand bed
- Concrete footings

CARPET

Wall-to-wall style is the best carpet choice. Select a weave that has a short, tight pile so the casters on your office chair will not catch. Commercial-grade carpet serves well; a showroom may have remnants from a larger job. This material is designed to take wear and tear. Avoid large area rugs; file cabinets and other furniture may rest half on and half off the rug.

Have the carpet installed by a professional. The costs of the pad and installation usually are included in the price per yard.

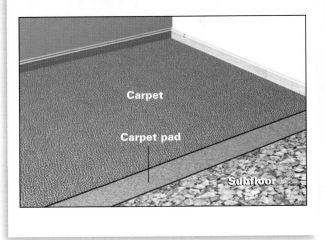

WOOD

Wood coated with a polyurethane finish makes a durable, attractive floor. Oak strips are the most popular choice. Most wood flooring is sold in tongue-and-groove strips 2¼ inches wide and ¾ inch thick. It is installed by nailing through the tongues into the subfloor. The subfloor should be at least ⅝-inch-thick plywood covered with 15-pound felt paper. If wood strips run parallel to joists, use two layers of plywood.

Wood can be installed over a concrete slab. Cover the slab with a vapor retarder and ¾-inch exterior plywood on 1×3 sleepers laid flat every 12 inches.

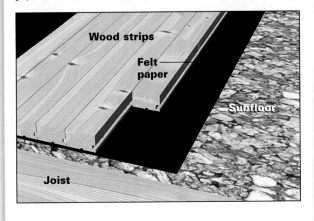

TILE

Tile floors tend to be more expensive but are strong and attractive. With such a wide variety of colors and sizes available, you can create a distinctive floor that complements the decor of the room. Ceramic floor tiles are usually square or octagonal. Four- to 6-inch tiles are commonly used, although 12×12-inch tiles may be more appealing. Preparation of the subfloor is critical because tiles are not flexible. The subfloor should be at least 1⅛ inch thick, composed of a layer of backerboard over plywood, or double layers of plywood.

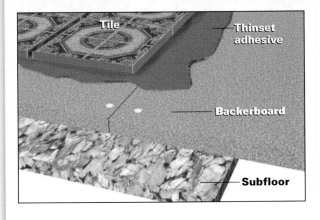

VINYL

Vinyl, the most common type of resilient flooring, is available in tiles or sheets. Both forms are inexpensive and easy to clean. Look for a medium to heavy gauge with a thick, clear-vinyl wear layer or topcoat. Cushioned vinyl is quiet and comfortable, but may not be suitable for chairs on coasters—hard-edged wheels can tear soft vinyl. Tiles usually come in 12-inch squares; sheet vinyl is available in rolls 6 and 12 feet wide. The subfloor must be smooth and even. Linoleum, largely replaced by vinyl, is enjoying new popularity, because of its natural composition.

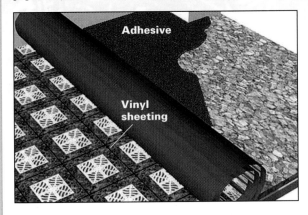

INSTALLING DOORS AND WINDOWS

Windows and doors can be purchased pre-hung in jambs you attach to the rough framing (*see page 34*). The manufacturer usually includes the measurements for the rough opening.

CAUTION: If you are installing a window or door in a wall with ceiling joists perpendicular to it, provide temporary shoring under the joists where the opening will be cut until the new header is installed. Construct the shoring 2–3 feet away from the wall and slightly wider than the opening you're creating.

Double-hung

Casement

Fixed

Awning

Sliding

Bay

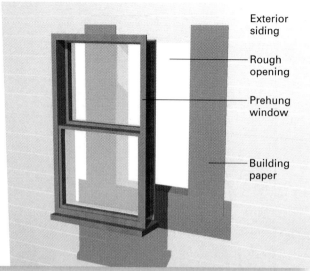

Exterior siding

Rough opening

Prehung window

Building paper

Windows are large and fragile, so their installation calls for a helper. With teamwork and preparation, a prehung window slides into place.

WINDOWS

On the inside wall, mark the rough opening dimensions of the window, then cut away a small amount of the wallboard to locate the studs within this area. Ideally, one side of the opening will fall exactly 1½ inches inside a perfectly plumb stud. If not, adjust the rough opening so that one side is exactly 3 inches inside a stud. If this places the window in an undesirable location, you can frame the opening in its preferred location, but it will require installing extra king studs (*see below*). Remove enough wallboard to expose the rough opening plus 3 inches on each side

from floor to ceiling. Nail a full-length king stud to the stud you originally chose. Use shims, if needed, to keep the king stud plumb.

Mark studs where they will need to be cut for the header and rough sill. Mark the bottom of the header at the same height as the other windows in the room. Measure up from this point a distance equal to the depth of the header and mark the cutting lines. To mark cutting lines for the rough sill, measure

Drive nails through shims

Add insulation

Shim to level and plumb

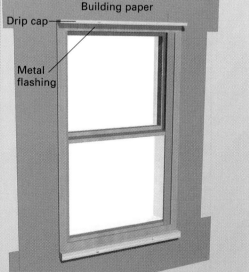

Building paper

Drip cap

Metal flashing

Take pains to get the window perfectly level and plumb. Drive shims where necessary to wedge the window into position, then nail it in

place. Insulate snugly to prevent drafts. Trim will frame the window and mask the rough opening.

down from the bottom of the header a distance equal to the rough opening plus the thickness of the sill material. Make sure the cutting marks are level. Cut each stud at both marks and install the header, trimmer studs, and rough sill. Toenail cripple studs, short lengths of lumber, to the header and sill studs.

Next, cut the exterior sheathing and siding until they are flush with the inside of the framing. If the siding is vinyl, you have only ¼–½ inch of play. The capping trim that will be installed around the window to match the siding is only ¾-inch wide.

Install the window according to the manufacturer's instructions. Use the recommended flashing and drip cap, and caulk the back of the window before inserting it in the opening. Shim the window plumb, then screw the window to the framing.

DOORS

Try to locate the hinge side of the door against an existing stud. Once you have located a stud, snap a plumb chalk line along its inner edge. Now measure across the wall the width of the door unit, including jambs. Find the closest stud beyond this point, and remove the finished wall between this stud and the hinge stud.

Using a circular saw with a carbide blade, which cuts through nails, cut the finished wall back to the center of the studs. Wear goggles; there will be a great deal of dust. Make sure the hinge stud is plumb, then nail an 82-inch trimmer stud to it. Measure for the width of the rough opening and install new king and trimmer studs on the opposite side. Stabilize them with a horizontal block, if needed. Install the header and cripple studs, then cut away the bottom plate.

Following the manufacturer's instructions, set the door within the rough opening and center it between the jambs. If you're adding a door to a new wall, install the wallboard to the edge of the rough opening first, then add the door. Use pairs of tapered shims to fill the gap between the jamb and studs on both sides of the door. Place the shims at the height of

the hinges. Check for plumb and adjust the shims.

Nail the jamb to the stud through the shims at the top hinge. Check again for plumb. Readjust the remaining shims if necessary, then nail through the remaining shim locations. Level the head jamb with a shim and nail it to the header.

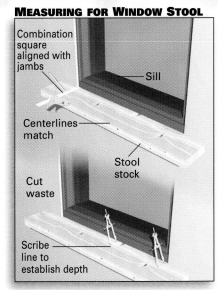

MEASURING FOR WINDOW STOOL

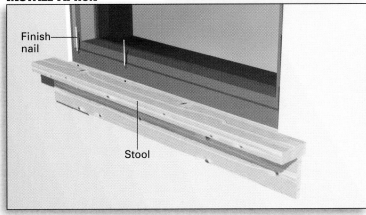

INSTALL APRON

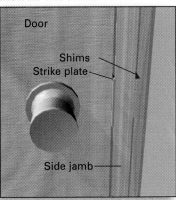

INSTALL THE LOCKSET

INSTALL THE STRIKE PLATE

TRIM CARPENTRY

Trim, or finish, carpentry involves cutting and installing baseboard and crown moldings, door and window casings, and picture and chair railings. The various forms of decorative trim cover gaps between different surfacing materials. Modern construction relies much less on trim because improvements in materials and techniques have produced more uniform, closer-fitting surfaces. Trim is still needed to cover gaps around doors and windows and between floors and walls. Even when it is not needed, it can give a room a distinguished look.

It is easier to paint a room before attaching the trim; likewise it is easier to paint the trim before attaching it. Once the painted trim is in position, all you have to do is fill the nail holes and touch up the paint.

INSTALLING BASEBOARD

Baseboard molding covers the gap between the bottom of the wall and the floor. It also protects the wall from being damaged by feet or furniture. Wood is the most common material for residential baseboards; commercial buildings often use vinyl or rubber trim.

One-piece vinyl sanitary molding is inexpensive and suits the minimal trim needs of modern buildings. With its slender profile and relieved back, it conforms easily to irregularities.

Wider baseboard is typically composed of three pieces. The baseboard piece may be a solid ¾-inch-thick board such as a 1×6, or it

Base cap
Baseboard
Base shoe

Drive finishing nails into bottom plate and wall stud.

can be specially milled to create a surface profile and relieved back. Tall baseboard is less able to conform to irregular walls and floors. The base cap and base shoe are more flexible and smooth the transition to wall and floor.

CASING A DOOR

The trim around a door is called the casing. It protects the jamb and rough opening from damage and gives the door its finished look.

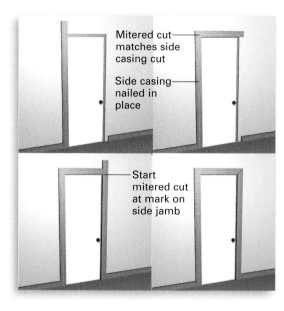

Mitered cut matches side casing cut

Side casing nailed in place

Start mitered cut at mark on side jamb

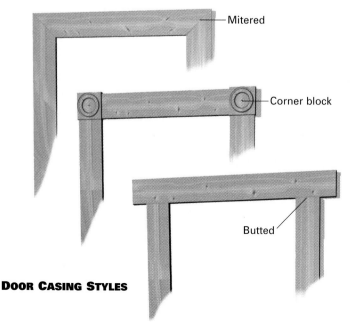

Mitered

Corner block

Butted

DOOR CASING STYLES

Door casing can be mitered, butted, or butted with corner blocks and plinth blocks. Choose a style consistent with the rest of your house.

MITERED SIDE CASINGS: Measure the side casing dimension from the subfloor to the intersection of the head casing reveal mark and the side casing reveal mark (the reveal is the ¼-inch gap between the jamb edge and the casing). Miter one end of the casing and square-cut the other end. Hold the piece in position to the reveal marks and check the miter for fit. Adjust as necessary.

If the finished floor will be wood, use a piece of this wood to scribe the bottom of the casing and cut at the mark. This allows the casing to clear the finished floor. For carpeting, allow ¼ inch clearance from the subfloor. Repeat on the other side casing.

When corner and plinth blocks are used, the plinth blocks are installed first. The side casings are installed next, then the corner blocks and the head casing.

HEAD CASINGS: Measure the distance between the outside edges of the side casings and, if applicable, add twice the amount of the head casing overhang. Position the head casing on top of the side casings and equalize the overhangs. If the butt joints are not tight, remove the side casings and adjust as necessary for fit and reveal. Fasten the casings with appropriate-sized finishing nails, spaced at about 12 inches apart.

A mitered head casing is installed like a picture frame casing.

CUTTING CROWN MOLDING

When cutting and installing crown molding, work around the room following this sequence of butt and cope cuts.

CASING A WINDOW

Make the first casing by cutting a piece of stock square at one end and a little longer than the final length. Position the squared end on the stool, aligning the edge of the piece with the reveal marks. If it doesn't fit, plane or rasp as necessary. When the fit is satisfactory, mark a cut line on the piece at the head casing reveal mark. Make a square cut at this line, position the piece, and tack it in place. Repeat for the other side casing.

If the side casings are to be mitered at the top, proceed as described above. Then tack the casing in place. Measure and install head casings as described above.

CUTTING CROWN MOLDING

Cutting and installing crown molding around the tops of walls takes considerable skill, but it dresses up a room dramatically. Your goal is to span from corner to corner with a single piece of trim, so cut carefully. Scrap pieces can be used around columns, or in nooks and bays that can be spanned by shorter lengths.

When turning an outside corner, you should cut miters. For inside corners, use miters or coped joints, depending on the type of wood.

On a coped joint, one piece overlaps and follows the profile of the adjacent piece. Hold two pieces of molding as they would be positioned on the wall and trace the profile of one onto the face of the overlapping piece. Cut with a coping saw, cutting slightly more material away at the back somewhat for a better fit. Adjust to ensure a tight joint in the front, where it will be seen, with a utility knife or file.

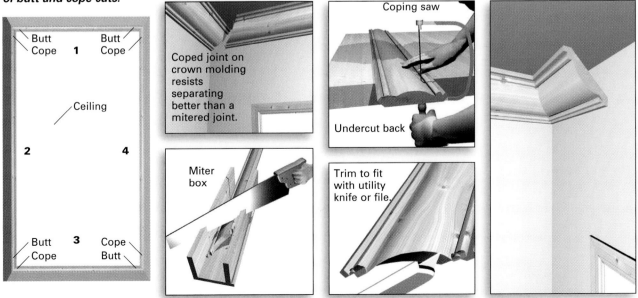

Coped joint on crown molding resists separating better than a mitered joint.

Coping saw

Undercut back

Miter box

Trim to fit with utility knife or file.

Butt / Cope **1** Butt / Cope

Ceiling

2 **4**

Butt / Cope **3** Cope / Butt

KEEPING SECURE

Working at home has its own inherent alarm system in that your presence in the house makes it a much less-attractive target. On the other hand, a home-based business can attract burglars if they suspect the presence of high-priced equipment or cash.

In about half of all residential burglaries, intruders enter through an unlocked door or window. Most spend only a couple of minutes inside the house. By keeping doors and windows locked and using interior and exterior lighting, you can significantly reduce your home's appeal to a burglar.

SECURING DOORS

A properly installed dead bolt or cylinder lock is an important deterrent. A good model resists efforts to force open a door and can't be cut through easily. Look for a unit with a 1-inch bolt, hardened steel inserts, and a reinforced strike plate with extra-long screws.

Double-cylinder dead bolts take a key on both sides, while a single-cylinder model has a twist knob on the inside. Double cylinders make it impossible for a thief to break a window and reach inside to unlock the dead bolt. But they are dangerous and prohibited by some codes because someone could be trapped inside the house in an emergency.

Dead bolts are usually installed 3–4 inches above the doorknob. In measuring for locks and marking the hole centers, always work from opposite the stop molding—the edge of the door. Stabilize the door by wedging shims under it. Install the lock or dead bolt first, followed by the strike plate.

Lock allows window to open slightly

Security bolt is tightened with nut driver

Keyed bolt

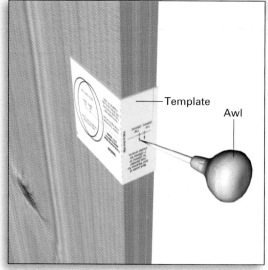

Hold the template against the edge of the door at the height of your layout marks. Use an awl to mark the exact centers for drilling holes.

— Template

Awl

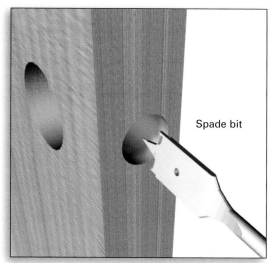

Spade bit

Cut the cylinder hole through the face of the door with a hole saw. Drill halfway through from one side and complete the drilling from the other side. Use a spade bit to drill a perfectly straight hole for the latch or bolt.

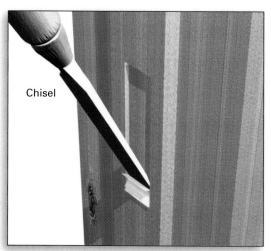

Chisel

Set the bolt plate and strike plate in place. Score the outline with a utility knife, chisel the mortises and drill the bolt hole on the door jamb. Fasten both plates with screws.

If the door does not have predrilled holes, you will have to drill them yourself. Begin by making a mark on the edge of the door 36 inches from the floor. Use a square to extend the mark across the edge of the door onto both sides. The holes will be centered on these lines. Install the lock or dead bolt as shown at the right. To find the location for the strike plate, close the door and mark where the latch or dead bolt hits the door jamb.

SECURING WINDOWS

Various types of locks are available for double-hung and other window types. You can make a simple security system by drilling a horizontal hole through the interior sash halfway into the exterior sash, then inserting a nail or dowel slightly smaller than the hole. (Many commercial window locks accomplish the same goal.) Some models allow the windows to be opened a few inches for ventilation but not any farther. Other window locks require a key.

Basement windows can be particularly vulnerable. Grates installed on the inside keep out intruders but can be removed quickly for an emergency escape.

THINKING ABOUT INSURANCE

One of the biggest mistakes you can make is to assume your home office and home-based business are covered by your homeowner's insurance. A typical homeowner policy may cover a few thousand dollars' worth of computers or other business equipment, but a fully equipped office may contain goods worth considerably more.

Running a small business, you have enough to think about without worrying about the prospect of uninsured losses.

Even if your home office is fully covered for damage, your income is not insured unless you make special provisions. Thus, if a fire or other tragedy makes it impossible for you to work, you can lose your income.

And your personal liability coverage may not be suitable for a home office that receives regular visitors. Talk with your insurance agent about upgrading your policy or about adding an umbrella policy to cover your home office liability.

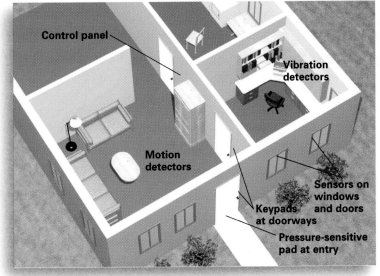

Control panel
Vibration detectors
Motion detectors
Keypads at doorways
Sensors on windows and doors
Pressure-sensitive pad at entry

SECURITY LIGHTING

Indoor lighting gives the impression that the home or office is occupied; exterior lighting can also deter a burglar. Keep security lights out of reach of potential burglars so bulbs cannot be removed or broken easily. Place exterior lights at opposing corners to eliminate dark areas which can become hiding places.

Photoelectric lights switch on automatically at night and off in the morning. Some models can be screwed into a standard light socket. Motion-detector lights turn on automatically when they sense movement nearby. They are a convenience for residents and a deterrent to intruders. Both wired and independent solar-powered models are available. You also can install sound-activated lights in particularly vulnerable locations.

WHOLE-HOUSE SECURITY SYSTEMS

Whole-house security systems are becoming smaller and simpler to install. Wired and wireless electronic models are inexpensive and come with a complete installation manual. A typical model uses a small radio transmitter linked to remote sensors. The sensors are usually installed at doors and windows. If the door or window is opened while the system is on, a switch sends a signal to the transmitter.

Motion and vibration detectors also can be connected to the system to detect footsteps. The sensors and any wiring should be as unobtrusive as possible.

DECORATING THE HOME OFFICE

Sparse elegance is the rule in this office where the few, classic furnishings play up the drama of the architecture.

A tall 7×11-foot room poses a challenge. To draw the eye upward, the mirror hangs high on the wall.

HEALTHY CHOICES: Plants can also protect your health. A NASA study has shown that many common plants can absorb household toxins, which is particularly important to people who are sensitive to certain chemicals.

Spider plant, bamboo palm, philodendron, and mother-in-law's tongue can reduce the amount of airborne formaldehyde released from plywood, carpeting, cleaners, and foam insulation. Formaldehyde can cause asthma and irritates the upper respiratory tract and mucous membranes. Benzene and trichloroethylene, found in tobacco smoke, plastics, inks, paints, adhesives, and synthetic fibers, are absorbed by the gerbera daisy, chrysanthemum, and peace lily. A typical office needs only two or three potted plants to reduce these indoor pollutants.

One advantage of a home office is that wall hangings, furniture, plants, and other details can be selected to suit your own style and comfort preferences.

OFFICE PLANTS

Plants are a convenient, pleasurable means of decorating an office. Clients feel more at ease, and work is less stressful when a room features attractive plants.

Trees look great in large offices. If space is a problem, smaller plants can be hung from the ceiling. Look for plants that are easy to care for and tolerate the light levels in your office (*see chart at right*).

LOW-MAINTENANCE PLANTS

TYPE OF LIGHT
- Low
- Medium
- Bright

RECOMMENDED PLANTS
- Boston fern
- Burgundy philodendron
- Delta maidenhair fern
- Heartleaf philodendron
- Prayer plant
- Swiss cheese plant

- English ivy
- Florist's chrysanthemum
- German violet
- Grape ivy
- Kangaroo vine
- Ponytail
- Spider plant
- Spotted laurel

- Cape ivy
- Earth star plant
- Impatiens
- Lemon geranium
- Painted nettle
- Swedish ivy
- Veitch screw pine
- Wandering Jew
- Wax begonia

SELECTING FURNITURE

Take time to peruse all levels— the high-end office furniture stores, the discount chains, and used-furniture shops. You need to see what is available, even if it exceeds your budget, so you can judge and compare. Be forewarned—a sticker on a piece of furniture that says it is "ergonomically designed" doesn't mean it's comfortable.

Don't accept poor design. Besides fitting you, your furniture should be adaptable to various work applications and compatible with other furniture designs.

For guests and clients, who sit in your office for short periods of time, look for chairs that are comfortable and attractive but not necessarily standards of ergonomic engineering.

A small table provides room for guests to work and gives you a separate work space away from the computer and phone. The ability to move around within your office can decrease fatigue.

Choose file cabinets with care. Whether you select lateral or horizontal units depends on the layout of your office. The most important parts of a file cabinet are the drawer slides. Look for full extension slides with ball-bearing rollers that work effortlessly when the drawer is loaded.

Office furniture doesn't have to be built in to fit in. This compact desk set offers a handsome place to work, with all the function you expect in office furniture yet it blends with the home's other furnishings.

SAFETY TIPS

Equip your office with a fire extinguisher and smoke detector, and check periodically to make sure they are in working order. Provide surge protectors for electronic equipment. Make sure phone lines to your modem also pass through a surge protector.

DECORATIVE FLAIR

You're free of the corporate yoke, so have fun with your home office. Your only restrictions are clients and conscience. Express yourself in the colors, background music, artwork, and plants—things that help new business associates feel at home in your home office. It isn't necessary to spend a lot of money on furniture. If you are just starting out or merely want to keep expenses down, consider building your own shelves, cabinets, and desk (*see pages 54-58*).

If you spend long days in an office chair, invest time in finding one that will support you comfortably and protect you from fatigue.

CHOOSING A CHAIR

A well-designed chair can make you more productive as well as more comfortable by preventing aches and reducing fatigue. It can cost several hundred dollars, but if you spend a significant amount of time in your chair, this is money well spent.

Modern office chairs are marvels of engineering. Their numerous adjustable features allow you to tailor the chair to your body. Heavily padded chairs may seem the most comfortable, but the best designs offer:
■ A curved front edge of the seat, which limits pressure on the backs of your thighs.
■ Padded, adjustable arm rests.
■ A back that can be adjusted up and down and in and out.
■ A seat you can raise and lower quickly.
■ A five-wheel swivel base.

Formerly a bedroom, this eye-catching office is stimulating as well as functional. A mix of upholstered and hard-line pieces provides a place to sip tea and entertain clients in addition to a place to handle the nuts and bolts of business.

DOUBLE IDENTITY

The easiest, least expensive home office is a modest work station set up in an existing part of the house. Many rooms can have dual identities, serving as an office when needed but maintaining other household roles, as well.

So, before you convert an attic or basement, or build a new structure to house your office, see whether you can design a comfortable, functional work space in an area that is used for other purposes or is simply underutilized. You can save a great deal of money if you don't need new foundations, framing, wiring, doors, and windows.

You may find suitable space in a separate room, such as a bedroom or den, that offers privacy and is out of the main traffic pattern. Or you may find that a corner of the kitchen or even a closet works. A family room, often the hub of activity evenings and weekends, may be a perfect office space during the week.

This chapter provides the basic information you need to transform a part of your house into an office, from building shelves and cabinets to adding an entrance and stairs.

BUILDING SHELVES

It seems at times there are never enough shelves in a home office. Fortunately, shelves for books, computer peripherals, and office supplies are easy to build.

SHELF MATERIALS

Solid wood shelves are strong and easy to build, although they may cost a bit more than other materials. Common hardwoods, such as oak and maple, are durable and can be finished to match other office furniture. Three-quarter-inch pine is usually available and inexpensive, although 1-inch pine (called "five-quarter" pine) is stronger. A big advantage of using solid wood as opposed to sheet products is that you can buy boards already cut to the width you want. The only preparation they need is sanding and a finish.

Sheet products, such as plywood, medium-density fiberboard, and industrial-grade particleboard, are considerably less expensive and tend to be more stable. You will need a table saw or the skill to make very straight cuts with a circular saw to cut the sheets to the appropriate sizes. Plywood usually is edged with a piece of matching wood. Fiberboard and particleboard can be painted to the color of your choice.

Shelf pins are sold at hardware stores. Several types are available, but most fit into ¼-inch holes

FREESTANDING BOOKSHELF

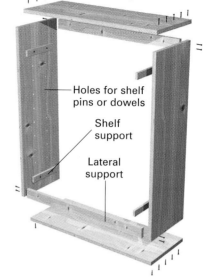

Attach with glue and screws

Holes for shelf pins or dowels

Shelf support

Lateral support

Attach top and bottom shelves to shelf supports with glue and screws.

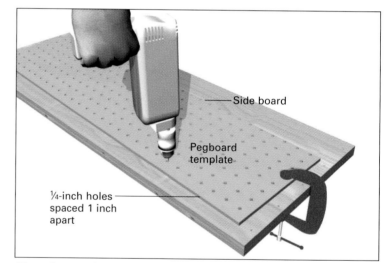

Side board

Pegboard template

¼-inch holes spaced 1 inch apart

To make evenly spaced holes (for adjustable shelf supports) on the side boards of your shelves, use a piece of pegboard as a template.

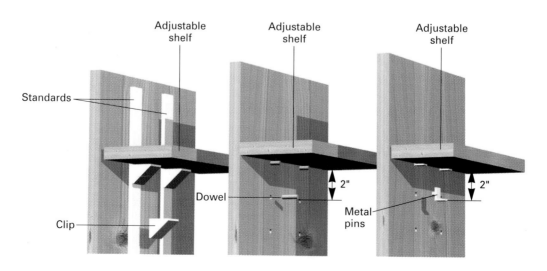

Adjustable shelf

Adjustable shelf

Adjustable shelf

Standards

Dowel

Clip

Metal pins

2"

2"

A library can serve the hard-working needs of an office and still be a handsome addition to your home.

you drill in the side boards. Four pins, two on each side board, are usually necessary to support one shelf.

You can make your own pins by cutting hardwood dowels to fit the holes. Or you can use clips attached to standards mounted on the side boards. You can use a router to cut dadoes—grooves in the sideboards—to recess the standards so your shelves fit flush.

FREESTANDING BOOKSHELVES

Freestanding bookshelves rest on the floor. They can be built to fit almost any space in your office and serve different functions. Floor-to-ceiling shelves can be made 12 inches wide to fit a small space, yet can hold a lot of material. Nominal 8-inch-wide boards, such as 1×8, are deep enough for paperback books, while 10- or 12-inch boards can handle larger books and notebooks.

Fixed shelves and or shelves with lateral supports at the top and bottom provide stability, while adjustable shelves offer flexibility. The side boards must be straight and cut to exactly the same length.

Drill holes for shelf pins before you assemble the unit. You will need two rows of holes on each side board. Space the holes 2 inches apart for shelving adjustability.

Drill the holes only deep enough to hold the pins; wrap a piece of tape around your drill bit so it cannot plunge all the way through. You can make a template to guide the drilling with a piece of pegboard clamped to the side board. The holes on each side board must align perfectly with those on the opposite board.

WALL-MOUNTED SHELVES

Mounting shelves on the walls has many advantages. Simple, inexpensive, flexible, it leaves the floor clear for other items and cleaning. Single-track standard-and-bracket units are acceptable for light loads, but double-track systems are sturdier and support much greater weight. The standards must be attached to wall studs. Brackets come in different sizes to hold shelves of various widths; you can even buy brackets large enough to support a fully functional desktop.

CLOSET SHELVES

You can turn a little-used closet into a storage facility by attaching 1×2s to the studs with 1½-inch-long drywall screws. Place one 1×2 horizontally against the back wall of the closet and make sure it is level. Then align 1×2s on each side wall and attach them. Measure between the side walls, then cut shelves to fit. Set the shelves loosely on the 1×2s, or fasten them with glue and screws.

Standards must be fastened to wall studs. The best way to locate studs behind the wall surface is with a battery-operated stud finder, an inexpensive tool available at home centers and hardware stores.

WALL-MOUNTED DESK

Heavy-duty standard

18-inch brackets can support a 24-inch-deep desktop

BUILDING CABINETS

Kitchen cabinet manufacturers have responded to the growth in home offices by developing cabinet lines for office use. Manufactured cabinets are more expensive, but you can trim costs by installing them yourself. Study the manufacturer's instructions before starting work.

You can also make your cabinets. It saves money, and you can build units that are the size you need. Don't expect professional-looking cabinets But with a little effort you can make an attractive addition to your office.

BUILDING BASE CABINETS

Base cabinets sit on the floor. Build a frame by attaching four 2×4s to the floor (set them on their edges, not flat). Locate the front of the frame 3 inches back from the front of the finished cabinet to create a "toe kick" space. Use shims, if necessary, to level the frame, and make sure it is square.

Attach a 1×2 ledger to the wall with screws driven into studs. The ledger must be level, aligned with the base frame, and 30-36 inches above floor level, depending on the height you prefer for a work surface.

Cut side panels from plywood or medium-density fiberboard (MDF). Trim the back edge to fit the wall and allow the panel to overhang the front of the frame by 3 inches. Attach side panels to the base frame and ledger with glue and nails or screws. Make sure the side panels are plumb.

Cut and attach a 1×4 countertop support to the end panels. Then install a divider panel, adding notches so that it fits around the ledger and countertop support.

Cut and install base shelves on the frame. Attach 1×2 shelf supports to the dividers.

The face frame consists of vertical stiles, which provide a surface to mount door hinges and horizontal rails. Make the face frame out of 1×3s. Begin by attaching end stiles with glue and finishing nails. Then attach the top rail, cut to fit between the end stiles. Additional rails can be added, if needed, to support drawers. Finally, cut the shorter stile pieces to cover the divider panel and add a board to cover the frame in the toe kick.

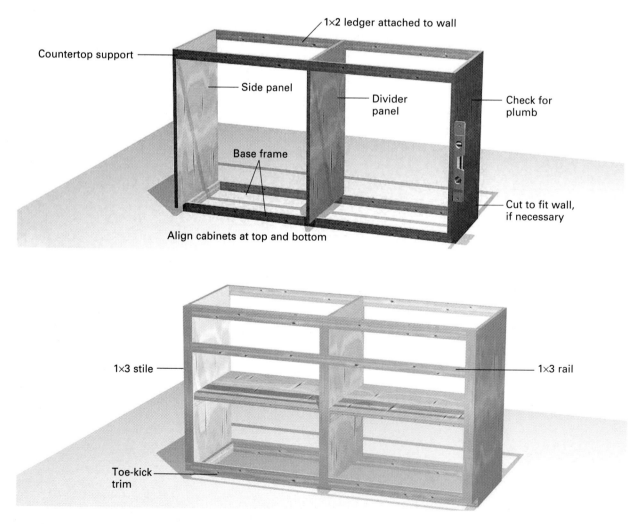

1×2 ledger attached to wall

Countertop support

Side panel

Divider panel

Check for plumb

Base frame

Cut to fit wall, if necessary

Align cabinets at top and bottom

1×3 stile

1×3 rail

Toe-kick trim

MAKING DRAWERS

You do not have to be a master of complex joinery to make perfectly good drawers. The four sides can be made out of ¾-inch plywood or solid pine, and the bottom is cut from a piece of ¼-inch plywood. Fasten the sides together with 1½-inch screws, and the bottom to the sides with ¾-inch screws.

The drawer face can be made from a nicer hardwood or hardwood-veneer plywood, or you can use painted MDF. Make the drawer face overlap the sides enough to cover the slides. Mount the face with screws driven from the inside, then attach a drawer pull.

INSTALLING DRAWERS:

You can buy good-quality drawer slides at home centers and through woodworkers' mail-order catalogs. Full-extension slides allow the drawer to be fully opened, while ¾-extension slides are more economical. For best results, choose slides with ball bearings and a load capacity of at least 75 pounds. Special-duty slides can be used to hold keyboards and file cabinets.

Drawer slide

Homemade drawer glides

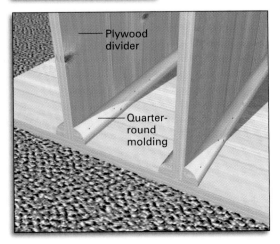

Plywood divider

Quarter-round molding

Install as directed by the maker.

You also can make your own drawer glides by attaching strips of solid wood or plywood to the sides of the cabinet to support the top and bottom of each drawer. Use dry wood and seal it well.

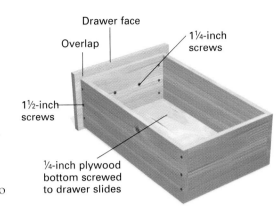

Drawer face

1¼-inch screws

Overlap

1½-inch screws

¼-inch plywood bottom screwed to drawer slides

MOUNTING CABINET DOORS

Make the cabinet doors from the same material used on the sides. Choose the hinges you plan to use before cutting the doors. No-mortise hinges are the easiest to mount—one leaf is attached to the face frame and the other to the back or side of the door.

Butt hinges are used on inset doors—that is, doors that set flush with the cabinet face. They require that you cut a mortise on both mounting surfaces in which to set the hinge. Use the hinge as a template to mark the outline, then carefully chisel the mortise. Use only one screw on each hinge until the door fits perfectly, then drive the remaining screws.

ADDING DIVIDERS: You can add vertical dividers to your cabinets as needed. Cut the dividers from a sheet of ⅜-inch or ½-inch plywood and attach it with quarter-round molding.

CHOOSING COUNTERTOPS

Countertops can be as simple or complex as you like. Plywood or fiberboard, finished to match the rest of the cabinet, can be prepared and installed quickly. Home centers also carry post-formed countertops, which are made with a thin layer of laminate over a particleboard substrate. Cut the material to fit, then attach it with glue and screws driven from underneath.

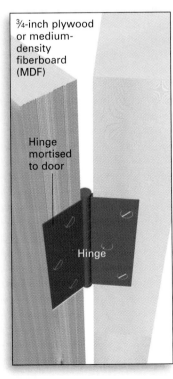

¾-inch plywood or medium-density fiberboard (MDF)

Hinge mortised to door

Hinge

BUILDING A DESK

SIMPLIFIED DESK CONSTRUCTION

Clinch nut plates allow to easily mount legs to tabletop

Steel corner braces join legs to aprons

Buy the legs or base, then add your own tabletop

Pedestal base

Folding legs

3-inch overhang on all sides

Traditional office desks are fine for writing and conducting business over the phone, but they are not as well suited for today's computerized home office.

Many people are happier working at a modified table with plenty of leg room and a surface deep enough to hold the computer monitor at a healthy distance. You can build table-style desks easily and inexpensively. The dimensions in the illustrations below are suitable for a full-sized desk top, but you can use the same technique to make smaller end or coffee tables. Adjust the length of the legs to make a desk top at the desired height.

Make your first table using pine. It is readily available, and mistakes won't be too costly. The top can be made with plywood, fiberboard, or particleboard.

The aprons are joined to the legs with dowels, and the corners are reinforced with a mitered brace. Make the legs by ripping a 2×4 in half. Use a plane to smooth and finish the legs to 1½ inches square.

Cut the aprons from 1×4 pine. Align the legs and aprons, while they are set upside down on a workbench. Set the aprons flush with the outside face of the legs or recess them. Drill two ¼-inch holes an inch deep in the end of each apron. The holes must be

AN OLD STANDBY

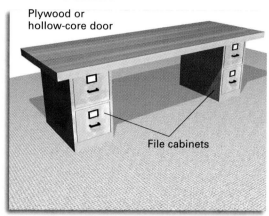

Plywood or hollow-core door

File cabinets

as straight as possible. Measure, mark, and drill holes in the legs to align perfectly with the holes in the aprons. Cut a 1¾-inch-long dowel for each hole from a length of ¼-inch dowel. Place the dowels in the holes and assemble the parts. If any hole seems out of alignment, plug it with a glued dowel cut flush and drill another hole. When you are satisfied with the fit, glue and clamp the legs and aprons. Check for squareness before clamping.

Cut mitered braces from a 2×4. Drill pocket holes perpendicular to the mitered surface, then attach the braces to the aprons with screws.

Cut the desk top to size and attach it to the aprons with metal angle brackets and screws from underneath.

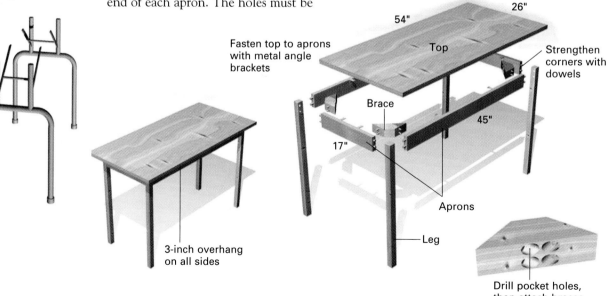

Fasten top to aprons with metal angle brackets

54"

26"

Top

Strengthen corners with dowels

Brace

45"

17"

Aprons

Leg

Drill pocket holes, then attach braces with screws

SHARING SPACE

Sometimes you have to find room for a home office when you really don't have room to spare. If building a separate structure is out of the question, you are left with two choices:

■ You can make an office that shares uses with another room in the house.

■ You can transform a nook or cranny.

Home offices that share space with other household activities present special challenges. The biggest problems are balancing competing uses, coming up with a design that integrates the two functions, and providing sufficient storage.

Sometimes, home offices can be set up in unlikely places. Imagine your house completely empty. With no predetermined notion of what should go where, think of a spot that is big enough to support the office you need. Perhaps that space is occupied by appliances or furniture; maybe it is serving as a spot for some item that can be moved. It could be at the end of a hallway, in a closet, or beneath the stairs. Once you've thought of the spot, think about what you can do with the items stored there to make room for your office equipment.

If you rejected the idea of building an office in the basement, attic, or garage, consider using those spaces more efficiently for storage to free up room in the house for an office.

A long closet can mean a short commute if you convert it to office use.

A dinner table serves as a desk, and cabinets stow office gear or tableware in this dining room/office.

The illustrations on this page offer two unusual, yet feasible settings for a home office. In many houses, the space beneath stairs is underutilized. Drawers and cabinets can be constructed to fit there.

A wide, shallow closet can be transformed into an office with plenty of storage and an ample desk top. One advantage of this scheme is that you can make the office disappear by closing the doors.

When all else fails, it may be time to call in an expert. An interior designer or builder with good design instincts may see other potential office sites that you haven't recognized.

The oddly shaped spaces created by stairs invite you to use imagination. For another example, see page 10.

BUILDING STAIRS

If you have made an outdoor entrance to your office, you may need to build a set of stairs to reach it. Or you may be required to upgrade the stairs to a basement home office. Building stairs is not difficult, but you must pay close attention to local code and safety issues.

MATERIALS

Stringers—also called carriages—carry the load on stairs. Short stairs, such as those to porches or decks, can be made from 2×10 stringers, but longer stair runs require 2×12s. Choose straight boards that are free of knots and splits, and use pressure-treated lumber for exterior stairs.

Treads on a basic utility stair can be made with 2-inch lumber—a pair of 2×6s laid edge-to-edge usually work well. Risers are optional, and can be made with ¾-inch plywood or 1-inch lumber. Fancier treads can be cut from hardwood tread stock available at most lumberyards. The tread stock typically has a rounded nosing and needs to be ripped and cross-cut to size. Risers can be made from square-edged boards of the same type of wood.

CALCULATING DIMENSIONS

Measure the rise from finished floor at the bottom to finished floor at the top. Use a plumb bob to get an exact vertical measurement. Divide the total rise by the ideal rise per step, typically 7–7½ inches. Round that figure up to a whole number, which becomes the number of risers needed, then divide the total rise by that whole number to determine the actual rise per step.

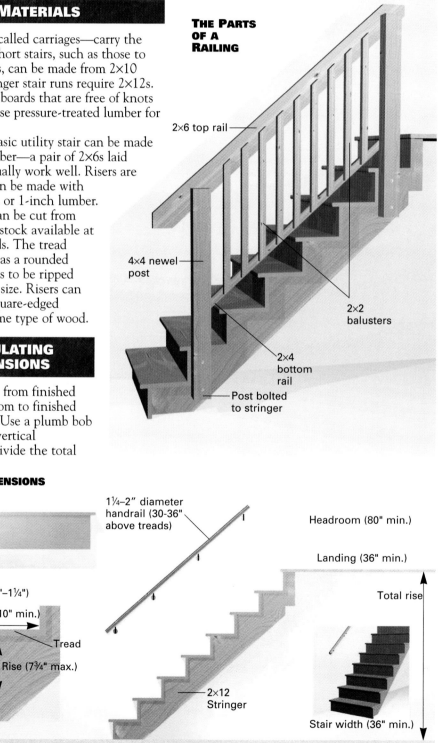

THE PARTS OF A RAILING

2×6 top rail

4×4 newel post

2×2 balusters

2×4 bottom rail

Post bolted to stringer

STAIRWAY DIMENSIONS

1¼–2″ diameter handrail (30-36″ above treads)

Headroom (80″ min.)

Landing (36″ min.)

Nosing (¾″–1¼″)

Run (10″ min.)

Tread

Riser

Rise (7¾″ max.)

Total rise

2×12 Stringer

Stair width (36″ min.)

LAYING OUT STRINGERS

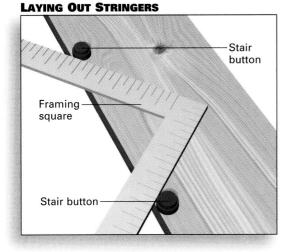

Framing square

Stair button

Stair button

Choose a tread depth—also called the unit run—which is typically between 9 and 11 inches. Multiply this figure by the total number of treads, which is always one less than the number of risers, to determine the total run. If the calculated run does not allow for an adequate landing, recalculate, using a smaller unit run.

BUILDING THE STAIRS

Use a framing square with stair buttons set at the run and rise to mark the first stringer. When the stringer is laid out, shorten the bottom riser by the thickness of one tread; otherwise, the first step will be too high. Cut the stringer with a circular saw; use a hand saw to finish the cuts.

Check the fit of the stringer; if it is acceptable, use the cut stringer to mark out two more stringers. Cut all stringers, then cut notches in the bottom to fit over a 2×4 kickboard, which should be attached to the floor. Exterior stairs should rest on a 6-inch concrete pad.

Hang the stringers from a ¾-inch hangerboard attached to joists or other framing. Drive 16d nails through the back of the hangerboard into the stringers.

Install a skirtboard on the wall side of the stairs, if desired, then install risers, followed by treads.

Build a basic railing as shown. Cut 1½-inch notches in the posts to fit over the stringers, then bolt them securely to the stringers.

CALCULATING RISE AND RUN

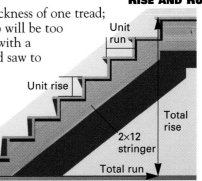

Unit run

Unit rise

Total rise

2×12 stringer

Total run

Make the entrance attractive and safe. Here, a bright red railing leads clients from the front door to a basement office.

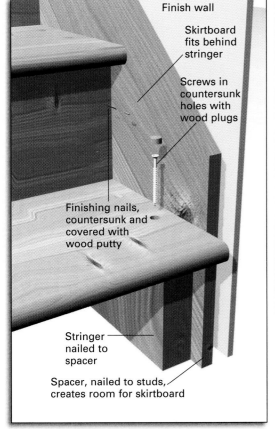

Finish wall

Skirtboard fits behind stringer

Screws in countersunk holes with wood plugs

Finishing nails, countersunk and covered with wood putty

Stringer nailed to spacer

Spacer, nailed to studs, creates room for skirtboard

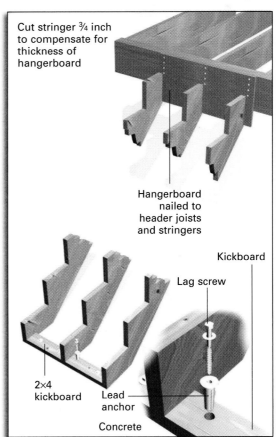

Cut stringer ¾ inch to compensate for thickness of hangerboard

Hangerboard nailed to header joists and stringers

Kickboard

Lag screw

2×4 kickboard

Lead anchor

Concrete

A PRIVATE ENTRANCE

Whether you are constructing a new entrance or remodeling an existing one, make an effort to design a comfortable, inviting face for your business. Use signs to direct visitors and specify whether they should walk in or ring a doorbell. Keep the entrance well lit.

INSTALLING AN EXTERIOR DOOR

Like interior doors, most exterior doors are sold "prehung," with the door already hinged to the jamb and the exterior casing in place. Both types of doors are installed the same (*see page 45 for more on framing a rough opening and installing a door*). Most exterior doors come with an extruded metal sill and an integral threshold. The sill must be supported on the outside edge as shown at right.

For protection from the weather, exterior doors normally swing inward. The jambs must be fastened securely to the wall framing. This is done best by nailing the jamb directly to the trimmer stud. To plumb the jamb on a prehung door, remove the casing on the hinge side and add shims until plumb. Attach with long screws through the hinge and jamb into the stud.

Add insulation around the door jambs. Caulk the threshold according to the manufacturer's recommendations. Install the strike plate and lockset, and add the casing and other trim (*see pages 46-49*). Caulk the joint between the house siding and entire door unit.

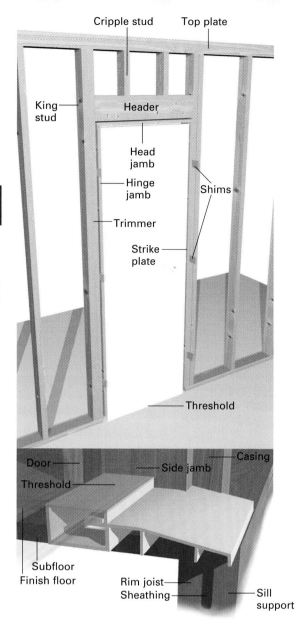

Cripple stud · Top plate · King stud · Header · Head jamb · Hinge jamb · Shims · Trimmer · Strike plate · Threshold

Door · Side jamb · Casing · Threshold · Subfloor · Finish floor · Rim joist · Sheathing · Sill support

SELECTING EXTERIOR DOORS

Modern exterior doors are better insulated and better sealed than their predecessors, which means they perform better and require less maintenance. Although construction and materials have changed, the most popular styles continue to bear a strong resemblance to traditional types.

Wood doors—plywood, composite, or solid wood—continue to set the standard. And wood-panel doors, consisting of rails, stiles, panels, and mullions, still define what many people envision as an exterior door. But

inexpensive wood doors can swell and warp with weather changes.

Steel and fiberglass doors are less expensive and hold up better. More expensive models are available with imitation wood grain. Be sure to check warranties when comparing doors.

If you are replacing a door, measure the old door carefully. Note the width of the jamb, which depends on the thickness of the wall, and whether you want the door swing to be left- or right-handed.

INSTALLING EXTERIOR LIGHTING

Exterior lighting adds security and showcases a home-based business. Low-voltage lights can guide clients to the entry to your office. A motion-sensing light turns on when someone approaches the door and turns off after a set period of time.

LOW-VOLTAGE LIGHTING: Low-voltage lights are sold as kits that include a transformer, cable, and fixtures. The lights may be controlled by switches, a timer, motion sensor, or photoelectric eye.

These decorative, low-cost lights can define walkways, highlight entries, and illuminate signs. If you meet with clients at night, they'll appreciate this cheery welcome.

The transformer reduces 120-volt household current to a safer 12-volts.

Mount the transformer near an outdoor receptacle and attach the low-voltage cable. Assemble the light fixtures and wire them to the cable as instructed by the manufacturer. Run cable between fixtures in a shallow trench unless the cable is likely to be damaged by foot traffic or a lawn mower, in which case it should be buried about a foot deep. Plug the power cord into the receptacle and set the timer.

MOTION-SENSING LIGHTS: For most residences, a detector that can be adjusted to sense motion 20–60 feet away is ideal. The higher the unit is installed, the less likely it is to respond to ground motion from animals and blowing leaves, for example. But don't place it so high it becomes ineffective or is too difficult to reach when a bulb needs replacing. It's also a good idea to keep the light away from windows in a location where it will not bother neighbors.

Run the wiring through the wall. Attach a watertight, exterior fixture box to the wall, under the eaves, or in an overhead porch enclosure and pull the cable through the box. Connect the wiring as directed in the instructions. Adjust the sensitivity to your particular needs.

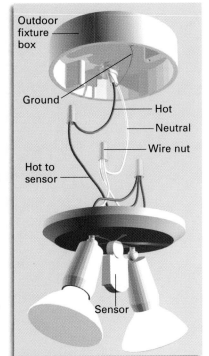

Outdoor fixture box

Ground

Hot

Neutral

Wire nut

Hot to sensor

Sensor

MAKING A SIGN

If you want to attract more clients to your home office, a creative sign often is the least expensive and most effective tool you can find. Check local zoning ordinances to see what kind of signage is allowed in your neighborhood. Your sign should not distract from the residential character of the surroundings.

You can avoid the commercial look by making your own sign out of wood or tile. To make a wood sign, you will need a U-shape gouge (a set that includes 3mm, 5mm, and 7mm gouges is best). Choose a fairly soft wood such as white pine, basswood, or walnut (avoid oak or southern yellow pine). The wood should be free of knots and straight-grained. You can carve the message into the wood or carve away the background to leave the message raised. Seal the wood with a good exterior finish.

Colorful signs can be made with small pieces of tile. Tile stores often have a supply of broken or damaged tiles that you can pick up for little or no expense. Choose a setting adhesive and grout suitable for exterior use. Break the tiles into smaller pieces with a hammer or use tile nippers for greater control. Dry-set the tiles on a platform of exterior-grade plywood. Once you are satisfied with the design, spread adhesive on the tile backs and set them in place. Wait a day or two before applying grout. Sponge the grout from the tiles. Apply grout sealer as directed.

U-shape gouge

Use straight-grained wood

Cut and broken tiles

3488

The homeowner still does laundry but in tighter quarters since this open area was converted to serve a home-based business. A walkout level provides two key benefits: ample window area and easy access. One challenge here was refining the tentacles of the heating system's ductwork.

CONVERTING SPACE

When you think of using existing space in your home for an office, your attic, garage, or basement may not come to mind. These are the hard-working extremes of the house, lacking in aesthetics and creature comforts. But don't rule them out—their open, unfinished nature may be just the opportunity you're looking for. To be sure, converting such spaces to usable living space is often a major project, requiring drawings and permits. Sometimes the work is so extensive you are better off building an addition or separate structure. But when conditions are right, an attic, garage, or basement conversion can be relatively simple. And, because these locations are isolated from the rest of the house, offices there may not cause much—or any—disruption of the household.

Dormers are another option. A cramped upstairs room can be transformed into a perfect office space with headroom and plenty of natural light. Dormers can also solve the headroom problem of an attic conversion.

CONVERTING A BASEMENT

Many basements are not suitable for home offices. Moisture, headroom, and access are often insurmountable problems. But when the conditions are right—or can be made right—a basement office is one of the easiest and least disruptive office conversions.

ASSESSING THE BASEMENT

Before you decide to convert a basement, check your local building code for regulations on basement remodels. Here are some of the common requirements you may have to meet:

Headroom for an office must be at least 7 feet, 3 inches, except under obstructions such as pipes and ducts, which can be as low as 6 feet, 6 inches. Don't forget to factor the added height of the finished floor and ceiling.

Basement stairs must be up to code. You may need to rebuild and reconfigure the stairs and the railing (*see pages 60 and 61 for more on stairs*). Simply adding a new floor will affect the height of the first step and that alone may necessitate a new stairway.

You may be required to provide an emergency exit, typically a window that measures at least 20×24 inches, located within 44 inches of the floor. If a garage adjoins the intended office space, a special fire-rated door may be required between the two spaces and the walls may have to be insulated.

Don't give up, however, if you are unable to satisfy the code. Talk to your building inspector about your plans and how to apply for a code variance. If granted, a variance will allow you to proceed even if your plans are not completely up to code. Obtaining a variance may take a couple of months. You stand a better chance of receiving one if it's not a safety issue.

To avoid the feeling of claustrophobia in a basement, get as much headroom and as much natural light as possible.

DEALING WITH MOISTURE

Moisture should be your first concern. If the basement isn't dry, or can't be made dry, it makes little sense to consider bringing office equipment and valuable papers into the environment. Walls and floors must be sound and dry year-round. There should be no cracks larger than ¼ inch and no water leakage.

If there are no obvious signs of standing water or other indications of high humidity, look for mildew or water stains under wood

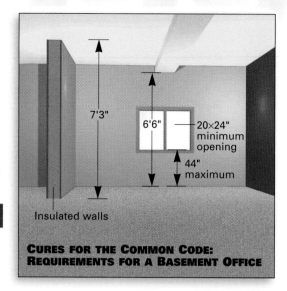

CURES FOR THE COMMON CODE: REQUIREMENTS FOR A BASEMENT OFFICE

7'3"

6'6"

20×24" minimum opening

44" maximum

Insulated walls

partitions, stair stringers, or floor coverings. If the walls or floor feel damp, even occasionally, tape 12-inch squares of heavy plastic at various locations below grade. Inspect the plastic every couple of days. If water is trapped on the back side, seepage is likely the problem. If water droplets form on the outside of the patch, condensation should be suspected. Remedies vary, depending on the type of problem.

Condensation often can be reduced by insulating cold water pipes, increasing ventilation, and directing bathroom and clothes dryer vents outdoors. Mild condensation problems can be controlled with a dehumidifier.

The primary cause of seepage is water runoff from the roof. Gutters and downspouts are intended to collect that water and direct it away from the foundation. But when they become clogged, corroded, or disconnected, the water falls close to the house's perimeter. Repair or replace any sections of gutters and

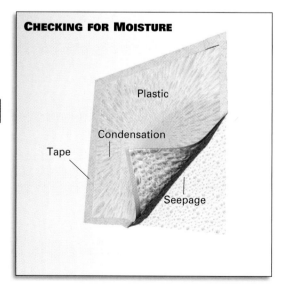

CHECKING FOR MOISTURE

Plastic

Condensation

Tape

Seepage

Clean debris
Patch holes
Gutter
Maintain slope toward downspout
Repair joint leaks
Downspout
Downspout extension
Splash block

downspouts that are leaking or disconnected. Clean leaves and other debris from the gutters every year. Gutters should slope gradually toward each downspout, and downspout extensions and splash blocks or leaders should be used to conduct the water away from the foundation.

Other causes of seepage include poor grading, leaking window wells, and damage to the house siding. Tree roots near the foundation often cause serious damage, leading to water leaks. If fixing these problems does not result in a dry basement, the foundation may need a perimeter drain. This is a job for a professional.

If your basement becomes wet at particular times of the year, it may be that the water table is too high. There are no reasonable cures for such a condition, although a properly installed sump pump could mitigate the problem substantially. It would be wise to consult a specialist before trying to construct a home office in a space that could face periodic flooding.

Basements without serious water problems can be given added protection with a crystalline waterproofing material, which is sold at home centers and lumberyards. These products are a blend of cement, sand, and chemical catalysts that you blend with water and apply with a brush. The catalyst penetrates the concrete, where it plugs holes and holds water at bay.

REPAIRING CRACKS

If you find water leaking through a crack in the basement wall, chisel out the crack to a depth of about ¼ inch. Run a bead of silicone caulk along the crack. After it has had a chance to cure, fill the groove with quick-setting hydrostatic cement available at home centers and lumberyards. Push the cement in tightly with a trowel. (Note that if the wall is concrete block, you should only chisel along mortar joints. Fill cracks in the blocks themselves without chiseling.)

REMODELING

Unlike attics and garages, basements need not be finished with new walls. If you like the industrial look, you can simply paint with special masonry paint designed to adhere to concrete and brick. Apply it with a roller.

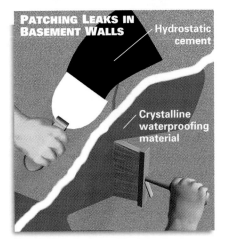

PATCHING LEAKS IN BASEMENT WALLS Hydrostatic cement

Crystalline waterproofing material

If you are not going to install a dropped ceiling, paint the area overhead white or a light color; bare joists can give your office a gloomy, closed-in feeling. Rent a paint sprayer and use latex paint the same color as the masonry paint used on the walls. Two coats probably will be necessary because dry wood absorbs paint. When painting, ventilate by opening all windows and using a floor fan.

If you prefer finished, insulated outside walls, give 1½-inch rigid foam to the walls between panels with construction adhesive. Seal the joints with foil tape. Then frame standard 2×4 walls, with studs 16 inches on center. This provides plenty of room in the wall for wiring and plumbing. You can finish the wall with wallboard.

Install a floor only after all moisture problems have been solved. Cover the floor with 6-mil polyethylene sheeting, overlapping seams at least 6 inches. Run the sheeting up the wall—it can be trimmed flush with the finished floor later.

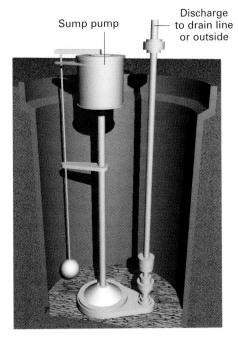

Sump pump

Discharge to drain line or outside

CONVERTING A BASEMENT
continued

Lay down pressure-treated 1×3 sleepers, wide face down, 16 inches on center. Fasten the sleepers with masonry screws or a powder-actuated gun (*see page 80*). Set panels of extruded foam insulation on the floor between the sleepers. Attach ³/₄-inch tongue-and-groove plywood to the sleepers with construction adhesive on the sleepers and in the joint and 1¹/₂-inch screws or ring-shank nails. Leave a ¹/₂-inch gap between the floor and the walls. Install the finish floor surface of your choice.

Alternatively, install ³/₄-inch wood strip flooring instead of the plywood.

Outlets in the basement will need to be protected by ground fault circuit interrupters (GFCI), required by most electrical codes. This can be done either by wiring the first outlet in a series of outlets on the circuit with a GFCI outlet, or by installing a GFCI breaker in the panel to protect the entire circuit.

You usually can heat the basement by extending whatever heating system is used in the house. If that is impractical, add a 20-amp circuit and install an electric baseboard heater.

AN INSULATED BASEMENT WALL

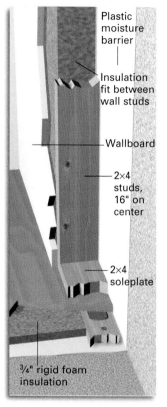

Plastic moisture barrier

Insulation fit between wall studs

Wallboard

2×4 studs, 16" on center

2×4 soleplate

³/₄" rigid foam insulation

INSTALLING A BASEMENT FLOOR

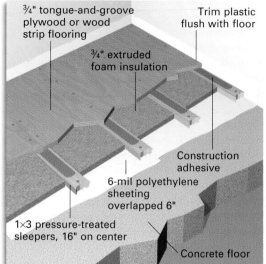

³/₄" tongue-and-groove plywood or wood strip flooring

Trim plastic flush with floor

³/₄" extruded foam insulation

Construction adhesive

6-mil polyethylene sheeting overlapped 6"

1×3 pressure-treated sleepers, 16" on center

Concrete floor

Although cooling a basement isn't usually necessary, it's good to have some means of circulating air. Window-mounted fans exhaust stale air and draw in fresh air through another open window.

If the basement is completely unfinished, construct a partition wall to separate the heating unit from the work area. You may be able to enclose the heating unit in a closet, but be aware that local codes are very strict on the ventilation around a heating unit and fire retardant rating of wallboard and doors. The door may have to be fire rated, so check with authorities before you begin construction.

A worker needs an occasional change of scene from a computer screen. When windows aren't available, as in a basement office, you can satisfy your craving for a view with photographs, collectibles, and similar objects to ponder while thinking those deep thoughts.

ADDING A CEILING

There are various ways to install a basement ceiling, depending on headroom and obstructions. If headroom is sufficient, a continuous suspended ceiling can be installed. A suspended ceiling has the advantages of leaving utility lines accessible, hiding sagging or uneven joists, simplifying the installation of light fixtures, and muffling sound. These ceilings come in many colors and styles, and instructions for installation are usually included.

Be sure that areas concealed by the new ceiling are insulated wherever necessary, especially in the rim joist area. Insulate any cold-water pipes to prevent condensation and dripping.

To install a suspended ceiling, mark level lines around the walls of the room at the height of the finished ceiling, which should be at least 7 feet, 3 inches above the finished floor. Use a long level or measure up from the floors, provided they are level.

Nail a metal molding strip around the perimeter of the basement, using the level marks as guides. Suspend main runners from the floor joists with screw eyes and wire. Space them 4 feet apart.

Fit cross tees between the runners to complete the grid. Use the slots in the runners for proper spacing. Slip the ceiling tiles and lighting panels into the framework. The tiles usually measure 2 feet by 4 feet and are held in place by their own weight.

RE-ROUTING OBSTRUCTIONS: Basement ceilings are often cluttered with pipes and ductwork that are unsightly and in the way. If the problem is merely cosmetic, you can mask the eyesore by covering it with a more

ADDING A BASEMENT BATHROOM

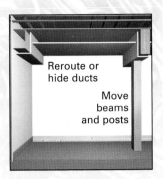
Reroute or hide ducts

Move beams and posts

Usually the toughest part of adding a basement bathroom is running the drain lines. It is easiest to add a bathroom in the basement if the main drain line already runs under the basement floor. That way, you will be able to tie the new sink and toilet drains into the main line by using a hubless fitting. To locate the main drain line, note where all the drains from above enter the floor, then find where the drain exits the house (usually on the street side). With this information, you should be able to track the path of the main drain. Use chalk or paint to draw the line on the concrete slab. Break through the concrete with a sledgehammer or rented electric jackhammer. If the main drain line is above the floor, talk to a plumber about installing a sewage ejector.

attractive material. Ductwork often can be moved from the center of the basement to the perimeter without much effort. You probably should have a heating and cooling contractor handle this type of work, since re-routing ducts can affect the performance of the system. Posts and beams are other likely candidates for relocation, but because of their structural importance, consult a professional first.

The most difficult obstacles to relocate are often the drain lines. Because they depend on gravity to function, drain lines must maintain a continuous slope with a minimum of turns. Sometimes, drain lines can be moved to run under the floor, but this is work that should be done by a competent contractor.

RELOCATING DRAIN LINES

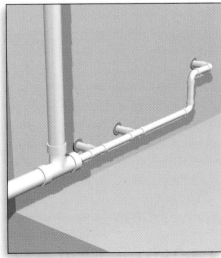

Exposed drain lines in the basement can be difficult to hide. Cabinets can conceal the pipes and add storage. The pipes remain accessible for plumbing work.

A more complex fix for this problem entails cutting channels in the slab to contain new drainpipes.

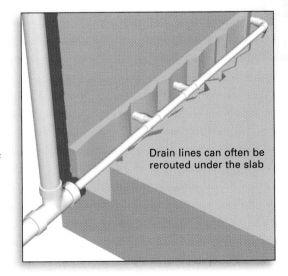

Drain lines can often be rerouted under the slab

TRANSFORMING AN ATTIC

Attics are generally not built to support the weight and functions of normal household life. But when you need more room and don't want to finance an addition or separate structure, an attic office can become cost-effective. As with basements and garages, however, it is important to assess the suitability of your attic before beginning any work.

ASSESSING THE ATTIC

Renovating an attic usually requires laying down plywood subflooring if no flooring exists, constructing kneewalls and partitions, installing insulation, and adding a skylight (dormer windows are another, more complicated possibility; *see pages 76 and 77*). Pipes that are

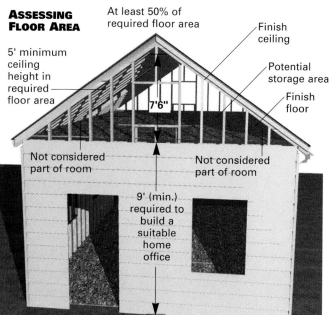

ASSESSING FLOOR AREA

At least 50% of required floor area

5' minimum ceiling height in required floor area

7'6"

Finish ceiling

Potential storage area

Finish floor

Not considered part of room

Not considered part of room

9' (min.) required to build a suitable home office

RAFTERS OR TRUSSES?

Traditional roof framing utilizes individual rafters that stretch from the top plate on the wall to the ridge of the roof. Roof framing on newer houses often comprises factory-built trusses, which use smaller pieces of lumber assembled in a network of webs. The webs of a truss should never be cut or altered in any way because the integrity of the roof depends on the integrity of each underlying member. A truss-supported roof does not provide attic space suitable for conversion to a home office.

ASSESSING FLOORS

2×6 ceiling joists cannot support a floor

2×10 floor joists (typical)

---

in the way can be re-routed or boxed in with framing and covered with wallboard. Wiring for power and communications should be installed before the wallboard is hung.

The most important things to check in an attic are access, floor area, headroom, and size of floor joists. Before you begin moving about in the attic, nail some boards across the joists to make a safe surface to walk or crawl on. Look for signs of water leaks and infiltration, such as damp framing, marks along rafters, or mildew. If a chimney passes through the attic, inspect it for water stains or creosote. If the roof is likely to need replacing soon, you might want to take care of that before beginning on your home office.

STAIRS: If your attic has fold-down or drop stairs, it can't be used as living space (*see pages 60 and 61 for information on building stairs that meet building codes*).

FLOOR SPACE: Also consider whether the attic will meet floor space minimums. Building codes usually define a habitable room as being at least 70 square feet, with the floor space at least 7 feet in each direction.

HEADROOM: The ceiling of the finished attic must be at least 7 feet, 6 inches high over at least 50 percent of the floor space. Do not count as floor space areas where the ceiling height is less than 5 feet. If your attic is unfinished, measure between the joists and ridge. If it isn't at least 7 feet, 7½ inches, you probably won't be able to convert the attic without substantial and expensive effort. Generally, you need about 9 feet of clearance

REINFORCING FLOORS

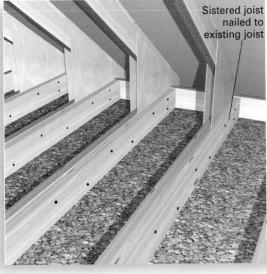

Sistered joist
nailed to
existing joist

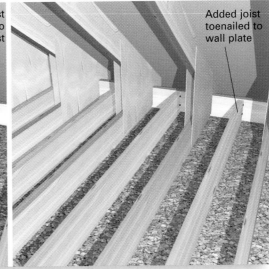

Added joist
toenailed to
wall plate

in an unfinished attic to be able to convert it to living space.

Collar ties are horizontal members attached to the rafters below the ridge. If your attic has collar ties that restrict headroom, talk to a professional about the possibility of moving or removing them.

FLOOR FRAMING: Floor joists must be adequate to carry people, desks, bookcases, and file cabinets. Ceiling joists are often 2×6s, 16 inches on center. This is not suitable framing for a floor and requires reinforcement. To determine if the floor framing is adequate, measure the size of the joists, the distance from one joist to another, and the span. Then consult code books or knowledgeable professionals to see if the joists can handle a live load of 40 pounds per square foot.

REINFORCING FLOORS

Reinforcing the floor in an unfinished attic is not difficult once you have determined how much strength it needs.

Ceiling joists, which are what you find in most attic floors, need to be converted to floor joists to support an increased load. You can accomplish this by sistering (doubling) joists or by adding joists. Before beginning, however, see if the joists are sagging; if they are, it could indicate a structural problem that should be investigated by a professional.

A sistered joist is fastened directly to an existing joist. This effectively increases the size of each individual joist. The sister typically is made from the same sized lumber. The new joist should be the same length as the existing joist and should rest fully on the same wall plates. Cut the ends of the sisters to fit under the roof and fasten the joists together with 3-inch nails.

Adding joists strengthens a floor by shortening the on-center spacing between joists. The new joists can be the same size as or larger than the existing joists, depending on your needs. Cut the joists to fit under the roof and toenail them to the top plates.

INSTALLING A SUBFLOOR

A subfloor adds strength and stiffness to the floor and serves as underlayment for the finished floor. Install subfloors before doing other work to avoid accidentally stepping through the ceiling of the room below. Plywood is the most commonly used material for subfloors because it holds nails so well. Waferboard, oriented strand board (OSB), and particleboard may also be used.

If your attic floor is already surfaced with 1×4 or 1×6 planks—a common practice before plywood became widely used—you may be able to attach plywood over them if they are flat enough and if you have enough headroom. Otherwise, remove the old planking first.

Subfloor panels, whether plywood or oriented strandboard, should be supported along each edge by joists or blocking. Alternate the orientation of the panels so joints are staggered. And leave a slender gap between panels to allow for expansion.

Subfloor panels
oriented to stagger
seams

Expansion gap

TRANSFORMING AN ATTIC
continued

Use plywood subflooring in a thickness matched to your joist size and spacing; the rating should be stamped on each sheet. Ask your lumber dealer if you are not sure how to interpret the rating stamp. Use the grade of plywood suited to the type of finish flooring you plan to install.

Square-edged plywood is the easiest and least expense to install. But all edges must be supported directly on joists or on blocking added between joists. For that reason, tongue-and-groove plywood is often preferred. The tongue-and-groove system eliminates the need for extra blocking, although it is always best to try and position joints over joists.

Stagger joints and maintain an expansion gap between sheets according to the manufacturer's recommendation. Orient the sheets perpendicularly to the joists, and be sure to place the best side up. Nail the panels to the joists with 8d ring-shank nails every 6 inches around the perimeter and 10 inches within the panel, or attach the panels with screws. Using a construction adhesive along the tops of each joist can reduce floor squeaks and nailing requirements.

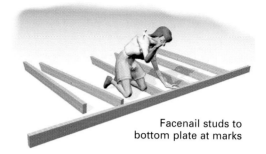

Facenail studs to
bottom plate at marks

is a convenient height for installing wallboard horizontally. Construction is the same as building a regular partition, except there is no top plate. Using a plumb bob, lay out stud locations on the bottom plate so they align with the rafters. Cut the studs and nail them to the bottom plate. Tilt up the framing and nail the bottom plate to the subfloor at the floor joists. Toenail the tops of the studs to the rafters, checking each for plumbness before nailing. Toenail 2×4 blocking between the studs for wallboard nailers.

BUILDING WALLS

The walls you build in an attic are not bearing walls; that is, they are not crucial to the structural integrity of the house. Attic walls can be framed like any other partition wall (*see pages 32–34 for more on basic framing techniques*).

Kneewalls are the short vertical walls that run under the rafters parallel to the ridge. Kneewalls should be at least 4 feet tall, which

Facenail studs to side of rafters

Nailers for drywall

Nail bottom plate to floor joists in position on marks

Mark stud positions with plumb bob and string

Tack bottom plate to subfloor

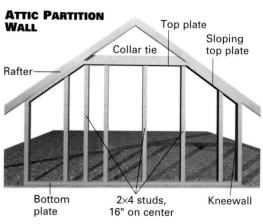

ATTIC PARTITION WALL

Top plate

Sloping top plate

Collar tie

Rafter

Bottom plate

2×4 studs, 16" on center

Kneewall

If the rafters are sagging or undersized, you can construct a structural kneewall to repair the problem. Talk with a professional, preferably a structural engineer, before proceeding.

WIRING THE ATTIC

Attic wiring generally requires three circuits. If there is existing wiring, use it for the lighting circuit. Bring up at least two additional circuits: a 20-amp line for an air conditioner and electric baseboard heater, and a 15-amp line for outlets.

Install outlets and receptacles as required by code

Run new circuits to the service panels, or extend circuits from receptacles in nearby rooms. Use fish tape to pull cable through the walls (*see page 36*). Cable that is run along the sides of joists should be stapled at least every 4½ feet. You can also run cable through ¾-inch holes drilled in the center of joists.

Track lighting and wall sconces are best suited to the gable ends of the attic. There also should be lights at the bottom and top of the stairs. Check local electrical codes for other wiring requirements.

ADDING INSULATION

Your local building code will specify the amount of insulation needed in your converted attic. Generally, codes require at least R-30 in the ceiling and R-13 in the walls. Install the insulation along the kneewalls and up the rafters. If you plan to use the space behind the kneewalls for storage, move the insulation back to the rafters, as shown in the illustration. Fiberglass batts are easiest to handle, but be sure to wear a dust mask, eye protection, gloves, and a long-sleeved shirt.

If insulation has already been laid between the joists, you can leave it in place as long as it does not protrude too far above the joists; the insulation will help limit the transmission of sound into and out of the office.

Achieving an insulation value of R-30 can be a challenge if the rafters are not deep enough to contain the 10 inches of fiberglass it takes. If you face that dilemma, consider using fiberglass batts in combination with rigid insulation nailed below the rafters. Be sure to add a vapor retarder, such as 4-mil polyethylene, on the warm side of the insulation, typically just above the wallboard.

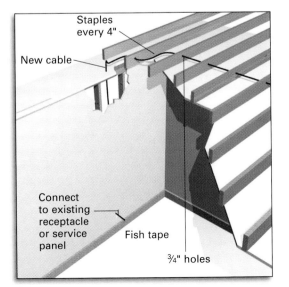

Staples every 4"

New cable

Connect to existing receptacle or service panel

Fish tape

¾" holes

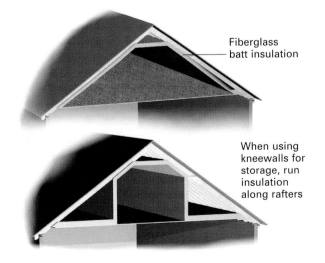

Fiberglass batt insulation

When using kneewalls for storage, run insulation along rafters

TRANSFORMING AN ATTIC
continued

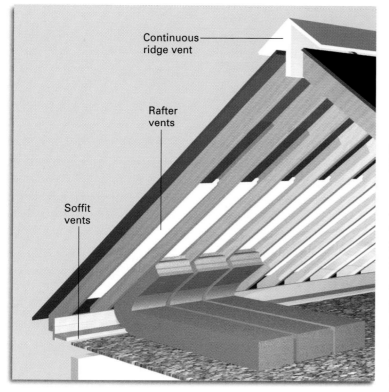

Continuous ridge vent

Rafter vents

Soffit vents

Allow room between rafters for air movement. Ideally, fresh air is drawn in through soffit vents, passes through rafter vents, then exhausts through a continuous ridge vent. Insulation must not block the movement of air through any of these channels. Other ventilation strategies can be used; check local building codes for requirements.

FRAMING A WINDOW

Installing windows in the gable ends of attics is usually an easy process. Because the gable walls are generally not load-bearing, a small window can be placed there in a simple frame. However, note that some attics are framed with a structural ridge beam supported by posts at each gable. Do not cut one of these posts without consulting with a building professional first.

To prepare a rough opening in a non-load-bearing gable wall, remove the studs from the window area. Mark the location and width of the opening on the bottom plate, then transfer this layout to the rafters using a plumb bob or level. Measure, cut, and install studs at the sides of the opening.

You may be able to cut and recycle the studs you just removed. Cut a header and sill to fit the opening and attach them by backnailing through the studs. Cut and install cripple studs.

Drill a hole at each corner of the opening from inside the attic, then go outside and cut through the siding. Install the window as directed by the manufacturers (*see pages 44 and 45 for more on installing windows*).

PROVIDING VENTILATION

Do not overlook the need for attic ventilation. Good ventilation exhausts warm, moist air that migrates upwards from the house below. It also cools the underside of the roof, which prolongs the life of shingles and helps prevent ice dams from forming.

Header

Cripple stud

Sill

ADDING SKYLIGHTS

Skylights will not add room to an attic office, but they can bring in sunlight and fresh air.

And if you're easily distracted by the view outside, a skylight can be the ideal office window. It provides light and a check on the weather, but you won't be tempted away from the billing report you're working on to watch the fascinating sight of your neighbor mowing his backyard.

Narrow skylights to fit between rafters eliminate the need for special framing. Larger skylights require framing an opening by cutting through one or two rafters. Fixed skylights cannot be opened and are easier to install and less expensive than venting skylights.

The most common problem with skylights is leakage. That is because of the tricky work involved in cutting away the existing roofing material and creating a new, weatherproof seal around the skylight. Buying a good quality skylight and following instructions carefully help to ensure a leak-proof installation. Installation procedures vary, depending on the model and size. If you are unsure of your remodeling expertise, this might be the time to hire a professional.

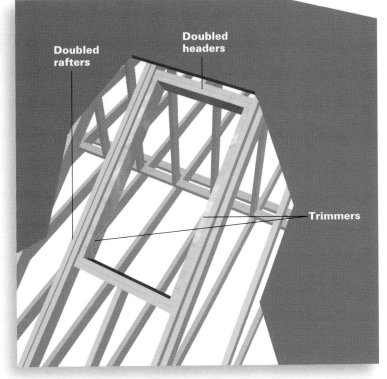

The higher you place the skylight, the more effective it is at ventilating the room. A lower skylight, on the other hand, may provide a more interesting view.

ADDING KNEEWALL STORAGE FOR AN ATTIC OFFICE

If space is at a premium in your attic home office, you can make a storage area behind the kneewalls—the short walls under the roofline. This type of storage is easiest to construct before you've installed the wallboard, but you can also add more afterwards.

Build shelves into the walls by preparing a rough opening much like that used for windows. Cut away one or more studs and install a header and sill to frame the opening. Build a shelving unit to fit the opening. Use ¼-inch plywood to enclose the back of the unit, then nail the unit into the opening. Add short studs, if necessary, to support the ends of the shelves (*see pages 54 and 55 for more information on building shelves*).

Small storage bins also can be built on casters so they can be rolled around the office as needed and stored in a simple opening without shelves built into the kneewall.

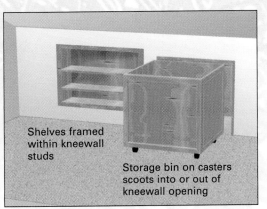

Shelves framed within kneewall studs

Storage bin on casters scoots into or out of kneewall opening

Kneewall space is wasted if you can't reach it. Simple, inexpensive plywood doors allow broad access to the shallow space under the roof's eaves. Whether you're storing office supplies or clearing space for your office, this is a valuable, low-cost opportunity.

BUILDING DORMERS

This 10×14-foot attic is divided into two rooms—an office and a book nook. A skylight provides much-needed natural light while a tall, narrow doorway flanked by leaded-glass windows shares the light and the view.

Adormer is a miniature addition. It adds usable space without changing the floor plan. Bright, airy dormers are particularly useful where low ceilings limit headroom or there are no other windows to admit light.

TYPES OF DORMERS

A shed dormer has a flat roof that slopes at less of an angle than the main roof. Shed dormers can be nearly as wide as the main roof and make a substantial difference in usable space. They are particularly effective on steeply pitched roofs.

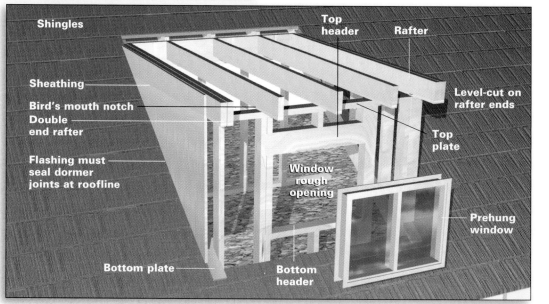

A window-filled shed dormer allows plenty of headroom and natural light into a formerly dark, cramped attic.

The size of a dormer makes it an appealing project for a do-it-yourselfer. But be very careful about seams. Leaks can haunt anyone who dares to violate the integrity of a sound roof. Be sure flashing seals every joint between horizontal and vertical surfaces.

Shingles

Top header

Rafter

Sheathing

Bird's mouth notch

Double end rafter

Level-cut on rafter ends

Top plate

Flashing must seal dormer joints at roofline

Window rough opening

Prehung window

Bottom plate

Bottom header

A gable dormer has a two-sloped roof that protrudes at a right angle from the main roof. The result indoors is a small alcove that admits light and provides room for a desk or other equipment.

FRAMING A DORMER

Be forewarned that building a dormer is a large project requiring a variety of construction skills. The illustrations on these two pages give you a rough idea of the steps involved in framing a small shed dormer. Do not attempt to do the work yourself unless you have experience in carpentry and remodeling. Also, since dormers are such a visible part of your house, consult a design professional unless you have a good grasp of architecture and can make your own drawings.

Mark the location of the rough opening on the rafters, then drive nails through the roof at the corners just inside the rafters that will frame the dormers. On the roof, snap chalk lines between the nails. Remove the nails. Score the shingles and roofing felt along the lines, then strip the roofing away. Remove the sheathing with a circular saw, setting the blade depth so it doesn't cut the rafters that fall between the rafters that frame the former.

Build a temporary wall before marking and cutting the rafters (*as shown at right*). Install the top and bottom headers with the top header, tilted on the same plane as the rafters, and add trimmer rafters on each side.

Frame the front wall, including a rough opening for the window. Cut and install dormer rafters, with a bird's mouth notch to fit on the top plate and a plumb cut to fit the top header. Use double rafters on each side.

Frame the side walls. Add sheathing, roofing, and the window. Carefully install flashing, then finish the project with siding, trim, paint, and caulk.

Remove roofing and cut the sheathing

Temporary wall

Front wall

Rough opening for window

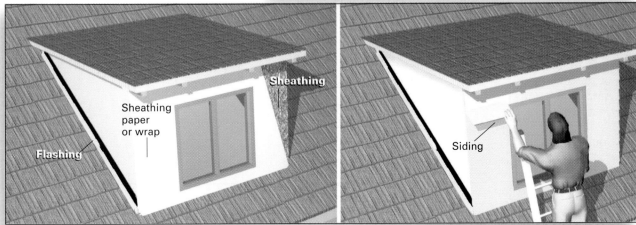

Sheathing

Sheathing paper or wrap

Flashing

Siding

CONVERTING A GARAGE

A garage can be turned into an attractive and functional office. From a construction perspective, garages are relatively easy to remodel because they involve fewer structural issues than other areas of the house. Most garages have open walls, so running wiring is easy. You may need to do some weatherproofing, particularly to make sure the floor stays dry, and you will need to install heating and cooling systems. A burglar alarm is also a good investment. Because the office is not in the house, it may seem like an easy target.

The obvious problem is that you now need a new place to store the lawn mower, garden chairs, bicycle, and other displaced articles. Consider building either a freestanding storage shed or a shed attached to the garage.

If you have a large garage, you can convert one side or even a corner to an office. Just constructing one or more floor-to-ceiling stud walls, and you may have to sacrifice the double garage door if you have one. You can then install a wall with a standard exterior door on the office side and a single garage door on the garage side.

You must avoid carbon monoxide buildup by making sure there is adequate ventilation in the office, and by installing a carbon monoxide detector.

Another project to consider is linking the garage to the house. An insulated, enclosed breezeway can become a hallway to the office. When you sell your home, the office can become another bedroom, a family room, or whatever the new owner wants to make it.

Before beginning construction, strip the interior down to the studs if they are not already exposed. Remove all lighting fixtures and protruding nails, hooks, and other items; hang temporary construction lights, if needed. During the demolition, carefully examine the garage and repair existing problems such as termite damage or leaks.

CONVERTING A GARAGE DOOR

Removing an existing fold-down garage door is fairly straightforward. Make sure the door is up and the tension on the springs is released. Springs under tension have a lot of snap and can seriously injure you. Remove the springs, unbolt the tracks, and take apart the assembly.

Next, build a basic frame wall with top and bottom plates to fill the opening. If you plan to add a doorway, frame the opening, while you are building the wall.

Before tilting up the wall, attach aluminum flashing and liberally apply premium butyl sealant to the bottom plate to reduce moisture infiltration. Next, tilt up the wall and insert it into the opening, tapping the bottom plate into place with a sledgehammer.

AN OFFICE ABOVE THE GARAGE

Sometimes the best way to turn a garage into a home office is to build upwards. This allows you to use the garage footprint without giving up valuable garage floor space. If the garage is attached to the house, you can make a direct entrance from the house to the office. A separate exterior entrance can be added for clients. The office shown above, built over a garage, has a separate doorway next to the garage door.

Before proceeding, carefully assess the structural integrity of the garage. The foundation, walls, and ceiling may have to be strengthened to support the added load. Consult a building professional and your local building department.

If you don't have a garage but plan to build one, consider building it with overhead livable space. You can use the space for an office. Future owners have the option of converting it to an income-generating apartment.

BEFORE

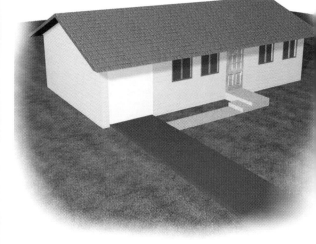

Fasten the bottom plate to the concrete floor (*using a powder-actuated gun or one of the other methods described on page 80*).

Think carefully about the appearance of your house's exterior once the garage door is replaced. Design and construct the new wall to look like a natural part of the house rather than an afterthought. Match window styles, siding, and landscaping. If the office entrance is located on a side wall, provide a sign and sidewalk for visitors.

PREPARE THE FLOOR

Concrete garage floors usually are sloped from the back to the front to encourage drainage. Garage slabs usually are not insulated, which can make an office uncomfortable during the cold season. The best way to fix these problems is to build a level, insulated subfloor directly over the slab.

Begin by cleaning and patching the floor. Use an oil and grease remover to get rid of stains. Chisel out all the cracks to loose, spalling concrete. Patch with fresh concrete. Next, apply a coat of asphalt emulsion sealer. Spread 6 mil polyethylene sheeting over it, overlapping each edge by 6 inches. Lap the edges up the side of the curb, if there is one.

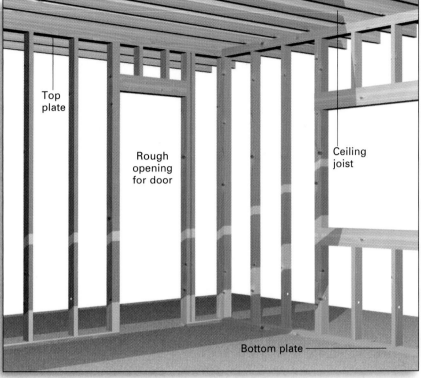

If the slab is relatively flat, lay down pressure-treated 1×3 sleepers 16 inches on center and fasten them to the concrete (or you can glue the sleepers to the sheeting using mastic, which means you need to put a layer of mastic on top of the asphalt emulsion first). For a sloped slab, cut tapered sleepers out of pressure-treated 2×4s and install them on their edges in the direction of the slope. Or, if the taper is modest, you can use wood shims under flat studs to level the surface.

AFTER The window line has been carried over from the house, tying the two together.

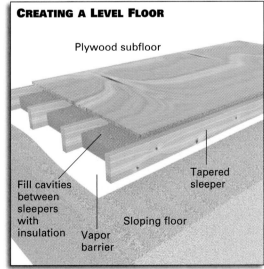

CREATING A LEVEL FLOOR

Plywood subfloor

Fill cavities between sleepers with insulation

Vapor barrier

Sloping floor

Tapered sleeper

CONVERTING A GARAGE
continued

If insulation is needed, lay ¾-inch panels of polystyrene between the sleepers. To increase the level of insulation, use thicker sleepers.

Attach ¾-inch tongue-and-groove plywood to the sleepers with construction adhesive and ring-shank nails or screws. Leave a ⅛-inch gap between sections and ½ inch around the walls. Cover the plywood with the flooring material of your choice.

RAISE THE CEILING

You also may want to consider raising the ceiling. You might need to raise the collar ties connecting the top plates to open up the space, and provide a uniform nailing surface for paneling or wallboard. (Generally speaking, the bottoms of the ties should be 8 feet above the finished floor.) A high ceiling also allows the installation of a ceiling fan, which circulates air and reduces heating and cooling costs. Raising the ceiling this way generally does not weaken the building significantly; however, get an experienced contractor's opinion before proceeding.

FRAMING A PARTITION WALL

Located over the garage, this architect's home office is readily available when the muse of late-night inspiration arrives.

You can build a wall down the middle of a two-car garage to turn half of it into a home office or add two small walls to create a small room in the corner of the garage. Either way, the walls are framed as typical partition (non-load-bearing) walls (*see pages 32 and 34 for more on wall framing*).

ATTACHING LUMBER TO CONCRETE

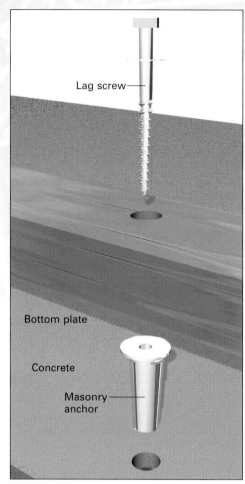

Lag screw

Bottom plate

Concrete

Masonry anchor

If you need to attach bottom plates to a concrete slab, you cannot use conventional nails or screws. The quickest procedure is to use a powder-actuated gun (or stud driver). These tools function much like a gun, using a cartridge to fire a nail into concrete. You may be able to borrow or rent the tool, although some areas may require special licensing before you can operate it. Be sure to get clear directions on safe use, and wear eye protection.

Well-equipped hardware stores and lumberyards carry masonry nails or screws, which are designed for attaching framing or furring strips to concrete. Masonry anchors are another effective means of fastening bottom plates to a garage floor. Drill a hole through the plate and into the slab, then remove the plate and insert the anchor. Replace the plate and fasten with a lag screw driven into the anchor.

Other types of masonry connectors are available. Be sure to follow the manufacturer's directions for the type you choose.

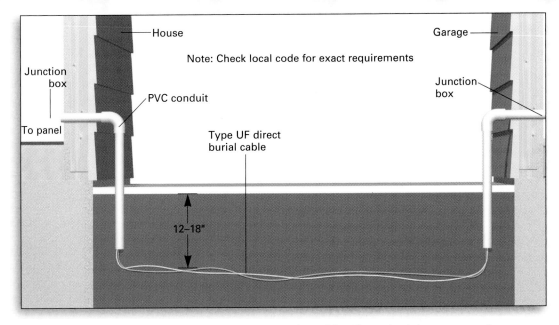

House

Note: Check local code for exact requirements

Garage

Junction box

Junction box

PVC conduit

To panel

Type UF direct burial cable

12–18"

Construct the frame on the floor, then raise it into position. Check for squareness and plumbness before fastening the plates. Attach the bottom plates to the concrete (*as described on page 80*). If you've built a level, insulated subfloor, nail the bottom plates to the plywood. The top plates should be nailed to ceiling joists if the joists and plates run perpendicular to one another. When the joists and plates run in the same direction, add 2×4 nailing blocks between the joists along with 1×6s to provide backing for wallboard.

Run the wiring and add insulation before closing the walls.

WIRING THE GARAGE

You probably will have to add or upgrade the wiring. Add a 20-amp line, if necessary, for baseboard heaters and an air conditioner, and a 15-amp line for outlets (*see pages 36 and 37 for more on wiring*).

Chances are the existing wiring is a single 15-amp circuit buried in underground conduit. This means bringing additional circuits from the main electrical panel in the house. Local electric codes vary on outdoor wiring. Some may require you to put cable in schedule 40 PVC conduit (don't use plain PVC pipe), or others allow you to use underground-grade UF cable without conduit. Some codes require a 2-inch concrete cap over the length of the run.

In most cases, you can dig a trench at least 18 inches deep to bury the cable or conduit. Use appropriate risers and LB connectors to leave the house and enter the garage. If you are using conduit, make sure to run a ground wire from the box out to the garage.

If you use schedule 40 PVC conduit, it will be easier to snake through the appropriate-gauge wires rather than trying to stuff through the cable. If you don't have to use the conduit, and can use cable, make sure to buy oversized risers to accommodate the cable.

To ensure your work meets the local code, have an electrician check your wiring to the box and make the connections at the box. Don't bury wires or seal walls until the work is inspected.

You can also use conduit in the same trench to bring phone lines from the house to the garage. Use heavy-gauge shielded wiring.

If the garage office is attached to the house, don't install receptacles back to back in the same wall space. Doing so would compromise the wallboard's ability to function as a fire barrier.

HEATING AND COOLING THE OFFICE

The easiest way to control the temperature in a garage office is to use baseboard or freestanding electrical heaters. An air conditioner can be installed through the wall or in a window. Depending on your climate, an openable window or two may be sufficient for cooling and ventilating.

A direct-vent gas heater may be more economical than electric heat if the office is used regularly. A small woodstove can be installed easily in a garage. Be sure to connect it to a properly constructed chimney, which can be run through the wall or through the roof.

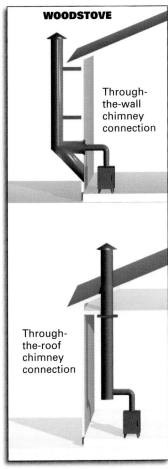

WOODSTOVE

Through-the-wall chimney connection

Through-the-roof chimney connection

This architectural office is located in space added above the garage. The office adjoins the upstairs of the home through a doorway.

ADDING SPACE

The least intrusive but generally most expensive way of creating space for a home office is by adding a room or a suite of rooms to your home or building a separate structure. This gives you the space you want, but costs add up when you include the help of professional designers and builders.

By building from scratch, you can design the space to suit your needs exactly. If business is booming and clients are visiting frequently, you can outfit your office with its own entrance, bathroom, and even a small kitchen, so work life and home life don't interfere with each other.

Or you can accomplish the same thing indirectly by building the new space to fulfill some other function. You can add a master bedroom or expand your kitchen, then use some of the newly freed-up space in the house for your home office.

DESIGNING ADDITIONS

An addition is a large and ambitious undertaking that requires a comprehensive plan and a professional attitude. You need to draw up a budget and investigate local zoning codes and regulations to make sure the project complies with local building ordinances. You may want to hire a designer and contractor for at least some of the work.

Another mortgage on the property might be needed to finance an addition, so the first step in determining whether you can afford construction may be finding out how much money you can borrow (for some loans, a bank may require a preliminary plan). The next step is to see how much you can build for that money.

Other new costs should also be factored in the increased monthly mortgage payments (higher insurance premiums, increased utility costs for heat and electricity, and increased property taxes). Knowing what these costs will be per year tells you how much your business needs to generate just to pay the "rent" on the new home office.

DESIGN CONSIDERATIONS

Building an addition onto your home is not only an exercise in creativity, it can provide an office that matches your needs perfectly.

Because plans must be submitted for building permit approval, an architect or a designer with a professional engineer's certification should prepare them. That means you must be able to explain exactly what your needs are. Pictures clipped from home and design magazines can help convey what you have in mind.

Access is one important consideration. A separate entrance means clients don't have to wander through the private part of your

Although the trusses in this garage-top office addition are not structural, they give a barn-loft look to the space.

Adding a windowed alcove made space for a desk overlooking the backyard. Portable electronics help this quiet spot turn into a busy, hard working office when business beckons.

BUILDING UP

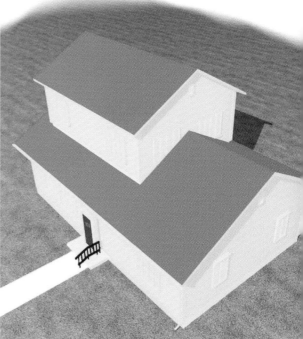

home. If the addition is on the second floor of the house or above a garage, exterior stairs can be added. If the addition is at ground level, a winding path leading to the separate entrance is an attractive option. Gardening magazines and books offer ideas on creating beautiful paths and other landscape features.

GOING UP? OR OUT?

One of the most basic decisions you'll have to make if you want the addition to be part of your main house is whether to build on top of the existing house or to add an extension. Often you don't have a choice. If your lot is small or setback requirements or utility easements prohibit lateral expansion, your only choice may be to build up. Likewise, if local ordinances restrict the height of buildings, you may be left with no option but to expand horizontally.

Cost often is a factor in this decision. Generally, building up is more expensive than building out because the lower floor must be reinforced to support

the addition. If your home's foundation and framing can support the additional load, which is not always the case, a vertical addition may be more cost effective.

Building out is usually less disruptive, since most of the work takes place outside the existing house. Building up creates a bigger disturbance but may help add life to a drab, aging house.

This main-level bump-out office reaches out to welcome clients. Its residential location is secondary to its business role.

BUILDING OUT

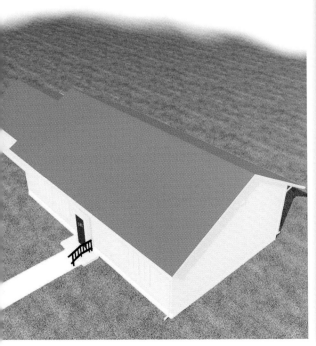

One objective of working at home is a work space that suits you personally. This writer's retreat rejects computers and corporate cubes in favor of a sturdy typewriter and a rich realm of redwood paneling.

POST-AND-PIER ADDITION

The advantage of this type of addition is that it can be built by an experienced do-it-yourselfer. Because it sits on a foundation of posts and piers like a typical deck, this addition can be constructed quickly and affordably. In many cases, it even can be built on top of an existing deck, using the foundation and framing that are already in place.

The 4×4 or 6×6 pressure-treated posts are set in concrete piers resting on footings below the frost line. Posts are set every 4–6 feet, depending on the size of the posts, soil conditions, and the size of the addition. With this type of foundation, you don't have to worry about digging a trench around the perimeter, ordering concrete from a ready-mix company, and having the truck drive through your yard. You can dig the holes then mix and pour the concrete yourself.

If your house is built on a concrete slab, it makes sense to extend the slab to carry your addition. If you live in a cold climate, you may want to investigate the heating benefits of building over a crawl space or basement. Otherwise, this addition can be built just about anywhere you can build a deck.

Consider hiring a helper, preferably someone with carpentry experience if yours is a bit weak. An architect or other design professional can prepare thorough plans, which may be required for a building permit, that tell you the size and spacing of foundation and framing components.

Light and height are hallmarks of new additions. This bright dining room does double duty as an airy office.

Many times, a new addition can be built on top of a deck, using the existing foundation and framing.

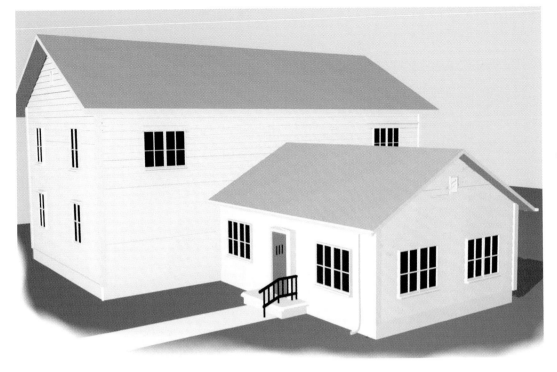

This post-and-pier addition turns the occasionally used deck into a regularly used home office. With careful detailing, the addition can look like an integral component of the original house design.

INSTALL THE LEDGER

The ledger attaches to the house framing. It should be installed level at a height that allows the finished floor in the addition to match the level of the house's floor.

Fasten the ledger with ½-inch carriage bolts extending through the house's rim joist. If it is too difficult to gain access to the bolt ends to add washers and nuts, use lag screws driven completely through the rim joist into added blocking. Use two bolts or screws every 24 inches along the ledger.

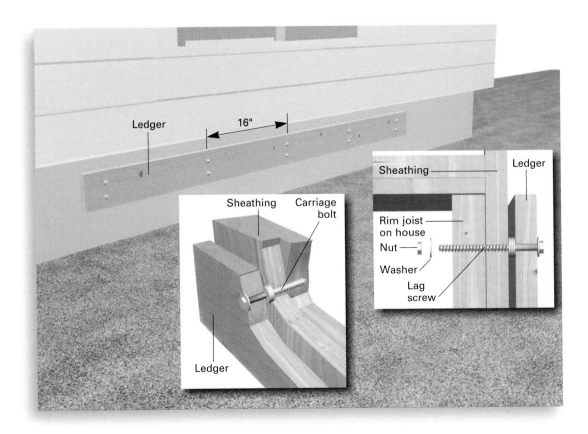

Ledger

16"

Sheathing Carriage bolt

Ledger

Sheathing

Ledger

Rim joist on house

Nut

Washer

Lag screw

POST AND PIER ADDITION
continued

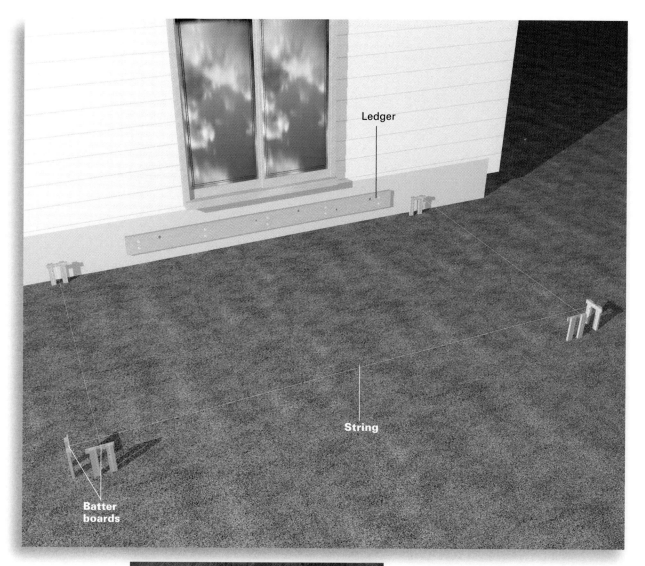

Ledger

String

Batter
boards

LAY OUT THE POSTHOLES

TWO-PERSON POWER AUGER

Use batter boards and string to lay out the holes. Batter boards are made from 1×4s, with two pieces driven into the ground and a third attached horizontally. Attach string to the horizontal board with a screw.

The outside string lines should mark the perimeter of the addition, that is, the outside face of the rim joists. Measure in from the string to find the center for each post, and transfer this measurement to the ground with a plumb bob. Stick a nail through a piece of paper or cloth at each post center.

Make sure the layout is perfectly square. Check for right angles and measure the diagonals of the layout, which should be identical. Keep the string lines parallel to the ground.

DIG IN

Digging even a few holes can be hard work. You can do the work with a manual post-hole digger. Ram the tool into the ground with the handles pressed together, then spread the handles apart and lift. Set the

MANUAL POSTHOLE DIGGER

dirt several feet away. Use a digging bar to help loosen rocks.

If you have more than a couple of holes to dig, consider renting a one- or two-person power auger. Hydraulic-powered augers are easier and safer to use than models with the motor mounted directly above the bit. Be sure to get an auger bit the length and diameter needed for the holes you have to dig, and take time to get a thorough lesson in the machine's operation from the rental store.

To drill holes in less time, hire someone with a truck-mounted drilling rig. Contact fence and deck builders in your area. The cost may be comparable to renting an auger.

Dig holes as straight as possible and keep the sides relatively smooth. For 4×4 posts, the holes should be about a foot in diameter. Cut a slight flare at the bottom of the holes and dig them at least 6 inches below the frost line.

SET THE POSTS

Place about 6 inches of gravel in each hole. Tamp it firmly with the bottom of the post. Center the post in the hole on top of the gravel. (Use only posts that have been treated ground contact.) Check the post for plumbness on two adjacent sides, then attach temporary bracing. This task is much easier with two people. The posts should be longer than necessary; you can trim them to size later.

Use premixed bags of concrete. Mix the concrete with water as directed on the label in a wheelbarrow or mixing tub. Add small amounts of water until you get the right consistency.

Shovel concrete into the hole and poke it with a pipe or piece of lumber to eliminate air pockets. Overfill the hole just a bit, then use a trowel to slope the top of the concrete away from the post. Check the post again for plumbness before moving to the next hole. Leave the braces in place until the concrete has cured.

If you dig a lot of deep holes, it may be worth having the concrete delivered by a ready-mix company. Calculate how much you will need and call for a price. Remember that the truck may not be able to get into your back yard, and if it does it may damage your lawn and landscaping.

BUILD THE FLOOR

Since the joists will be fairly close to the ground, use pressure-treated lumber. Carefully mark and cut the posts so that they are at the same height you want the tops of the joists. Attach the rim joists to the outsides of the posts. The joists can be held in place temporarily with a nail or screw. Be sure the joists are level, then fasten them to posts permanently with ½-inch carriage bolts. Use joist hangers for the side joists.

Measure and mark a joist layout on the ledger and the outside rim joist. Attach joists with joist hangers. Use the nails or screws

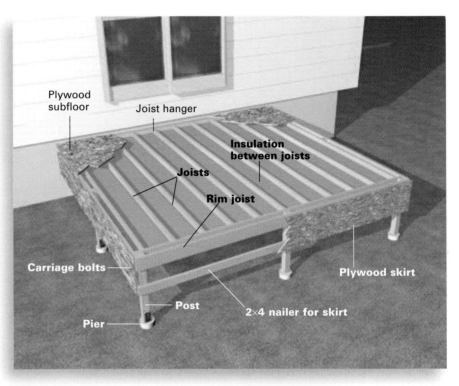

specified by the hanger manufacturer. Keep the tops of the joists on the same plane as the rim joists and install them with the crown pointing up.

Cover the bottom of the joists with screening or hardware cloth to keep out insects and rodents. Cover the ground with 6-mil black plastic (remove the sod first, if you like).

Run heating and cooling ducts into the addition, if necessary. Fill the spaces between joists with fiberglass insulation. If required, install crawlspace vents.

Attach a ¾-inch tongue-and-groove plywood subfloor to the joists with construction adhesive and nails.

POST AND PIER ADDITION
continued

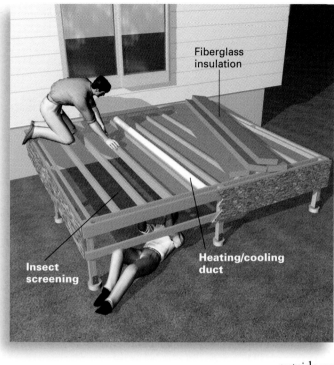

Fiberglass insulation

Insect screening

Heating/cooling duct

surface for your circular saw. Set the blade depth so that it doesn't cut into the sheathing.

The ridge beam for the addition needs to be attached to the house framing. The details for this connection should be worked out by a professional. Cut through the sheathing to create a pocket for the beam.

Frame one side wall on the deck, then raise it into position (*see pages 32-34 for more on framing*). Attach temporary blocks to the rim joist to locate the raised wall and keep it from slipping over the side. Plumb the wall with a level while a helper attaches temporary bracing. Frame and raise the other side wall, then build the outside wall to fit between the side walls. The outside wall will require a built-up post to support the ridge beam. Verify that walls are plumb and square, then fasten them to the floor framing, house sheathing, and one another. Cut and install the doubled top plate to overlap at the corners, as shown below.

FRAME THE WALLS

Mark the outline of the addition on the siding of the house. Carefully cut through and remove the siding.

To cut beveled siding, nail a long 1×4 perpendicular to the siding to serve as a flat

FRAME THE ROOF

Install the ridge beam, then mark a rafter layout on both sides of the beam and on tops of the wall plates. (Note: If you make the beam using several pieces of lumber, it will be easier to lift and install each piece individually than if you have a solid beam. Still, you may want to rent scaffolding for the day to make this job safer and easier.)

Lay out and cut the rafters. Make plumb cuts at the ridge and the tail and a bird's-mouth notch to fit over the top plate. Attach the rafters. Be sure to add rafters to the house sheathing, driving the nails into the house's framing.

Don't cut corners when framing corners. Take plenty of time to make your frame faultlessly plumb and square. Double up the top plate and corner posts. Then reinforce the studs with blocking and spacers.

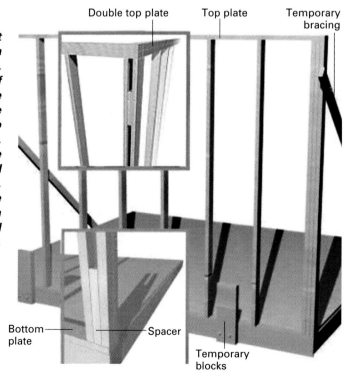

Double top plate

Top plate

Temporary bracing

Bottom plate

Spacer

Temporary blocks

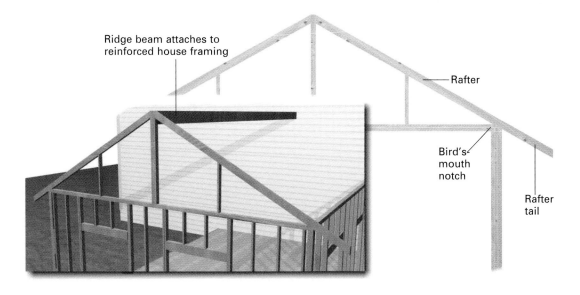

Ridge beam attaches to reinforced house framing

Rafter

Bird's mouth notch

Rafter tail

SHEATHE AND FINISH

Sheathe the roof and walls with plywood. Add a skirt of pressure-treated plywood to cover the crawl space below the wall sheathing. Nail the top of the skirt to the rim joist and the bottom to 2×4 pressure-treated nailers attached to the posts.

The skirt allows you to install siding almost to grade. You also may want to add a finish that resembles the foundation of the rest of the house.

Add roofing, with step flashing at the junction of the roof and wall of the existing house. Add ridge and soffit vents, if required. Install windows and an exterior door. Install trim around the door, windows, and at the fascia and rake. Finish the exterior by installing siding, painting or staining to match the house, and building stairs.

On the inside, run wiring, insulate the walls and ceiling, then enclose and finish the walls.

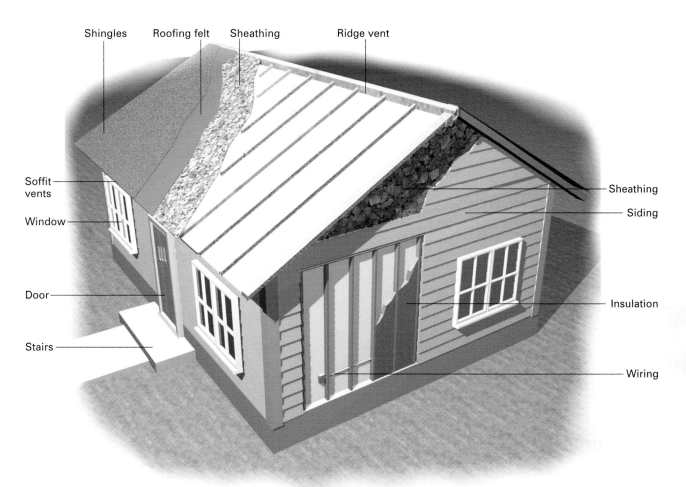

Shingles Roofing felt Sheathing Ridge vent

Soffit vents

Window

Door

Stairs

Sheathing

Siding

Insulation

Wiring

CREATING A DETACHED OFFICE

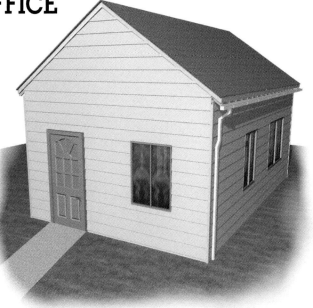

A small, detached office has many of the advantages of a garage conversion, including a separate ground-floor entrance. Large home centers sell prefabricated sheds you can convert to office use with a little effort. And some companies are capitalizing on the popularity of home offices by making small office structures that can be delivered to your backyard. If you are contemplating building a separate structure for your home office, it is worth shopping around to see what kinds of units are available.

You'll keep your frustration and expense down if you stick with simple forms. You can make an office building like the one at right by starting with plans for a standard garage.

If you would rather build your own, here is one simple design most do-it-yourselfers can tackle. This structure rests on a concrete slab, but you can also use a post-and-pier foundation (*see pages 86-91*). It can also be constructed as an addition, sharing a wall with the house or garage.

It's wise to check local zoning laws before building a detached office on your property. The usual setback for such a building is at least 5 feet from the property line. A building permit may be needed for a structure exceeding a certain square footage.

Footings must extend below the local frost line. Pour a concrete slab 3–4 inches thick over a bed consisting of 4 inches of gravel and 2 inches of sand.

When evaluating your property for a separate structure, consider its security—building an office in a remote corner of your lot may be an invitation to a burglar.

PREPARE THE SLAB

A concrete slab foundation is composed of a series of layers. Specific dimensions and materials depend on the soil conditions, climate, and size of the structure. Check your local code for exact requirements.

A typical slab for a small structure consists of 3–4 inches of concrete poured over at least 4 inches of compacted gravel. The slab is reinforced with rebar or welded wire mesh. A concrete-rated moisture barrier separates the two layers. A 2-inch layer of sand between the concrete and the moisture barrier is often recommended for a stronger slab.

The perimeter is a turned-down footing that is a wider and deeper extension of the slab. The footing is reinforced with rebar. Slabs lose most of their heat at the perimeter, so unless you live in a warm climate, you should cover the outside of the footing with rigid insulation.

If you are required to have a deeper footing, you will have to pour it separately. Because of the extra work involved, you may want to have a concrete contractor do the work.

Set up batter boards and strings to mark the outline of the slab. Excavate the slab area deep enough so that the surface will be at least 2 inches above ground level. Dig the footing trench wide enough to allow room for the forms. You may be required to compact the soil or treat it to ward off termites.

Using the string lines and a plumb bob as guides, set up 2× form boards in the trench. Nail the boards to 2×4 stakes driven into the trench every 2 feet. Brace the corners with extra stakes. Add the gravel and moisture

EXCAVATE FOR SLAB

Batter boards

Trench for footing

String

barrier, and sand, if needed. Place metal reinforcement in the excavated area; use bricks or stones to prop it up in the middle of the slab. Add rebar to the footing.

Dampen the soil and oil the sides of the forms. Have one or more helpers when the ready-mix truck arrives. Work the concrete into the trench; use a rake or hoe to spread it evenly. If necessary, use the rake to reposition the reinforcement if it shifts.

Use a 2×4 to screed (level) the concrete. Tamp it, then smooth it with a bull float. Use a wooden float or trowel to finish the surface. Install anchor bolts while the concrete is still wet. Allow the slab to cure for at least a week.

FRAME AND RAISE WALLS

Frame the walls on the slab, beginning with the longest ones. Drill holes in the sills to fit over the anchor bolts. When all walls have been raised and braced, fasten the sills to the slab with washers and nuts. Tie the tops of the walls together with double top plates (*see pages 32-34 and 86-91 for further details*).

INSTALL ROOF TRUSSES

Prefabricated roof trusses are quicker to install than rafters you frame yourself. Order the trusses several weeks in advance. The manufacturer will need to know the dimensions of your structure and the pitch of the roof. You also can specify the overhang desired on the eaves and rake. Make sure the manufacturer supplies complete instructions. You will need a helper to erect the trusses.

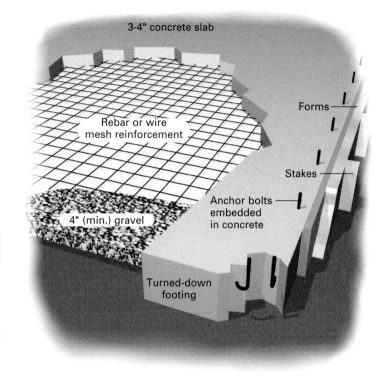

3-4" concrete slab

Rebar or wire mesh reinforcement

Forms

Stakes

Anchor bolts embedded in concrete

4" (min.) gravel

Turned-down footing

ADD THE SIDING

You can side your new office with any material used for house siding. Textured plywood siding is a good choice because it is inexpensive, sturdy, and easy to install. Many patterns and textures are available. Plywood siding can be attached directly to the studs and doesn't require extra bracing or a separate layer of sheathing.

The siding is available in 4-foot-wide panels, in lengths of 8–10 feet. The panels are usually installed vertically, with the edges falling on wall studs. Any horizontal joints require extra blocking as well as flashing.

Follow the manufacturer's advice on leaving expansion gaps at panel edges, and treat the edges with water repellent before installing them. Expansion gaps can be caulked or covered with vertical battens. Don't bring the panels all the way down to ground level; some products require a 3-inch separation.

Snap a level chalk line on the slab to help align the bottom edges of the panels. Place the first panel flush with a corner of the structure, with the other side centered on a stud. Use and space the fasteners as recommended by the manufacturer.

A concrete slab provides a firm, smooth, and enduring base. Your results depend on the preparation: square forms, a bed of gravel, steel reinforcing, and embedded anchor bolts.

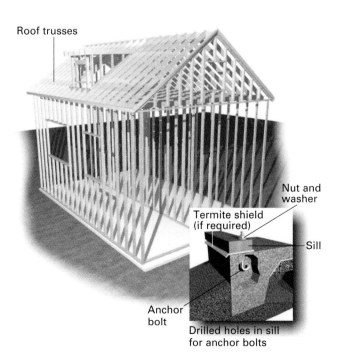

Roof trusses

Nut and washer

Termite shield (if required)

Sill

Anchor bolt

Drilled holes in sill for anchor bolts

A DETACHED OFFICE

continued

To hasten installation, cover the entire structure with siding, then go back and cut out the rough openings for windows and a door. Add trim at the corners and around the door and windows.

INSTALL ROOFING

As with the siding, many roofing options are available. Asphalt shingles are the most obvious. For a small and simple structure like this, however, you might want to take a little extra time to install cedar shingles. Standard cedar shingles are 16 inches long and sold in random widths. Buy the highest grade available. Install the shingles over 1×3 wooden strips—called skip sheathing—attached perpendicularly to rafters or trusses. The spacing between the strips is dictated by the shingle exposure. For speedier installation, look for prefabricated panels of shingles.

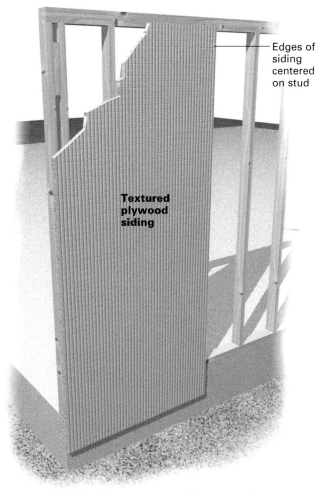

Edges of siding centered on stud

Textured plywood siding

Skip sheathing

Panel siding goes up quickly and easily. Its tongue-and-groove edges fit together snugly. You can measure and cut door and window openings before installing panels or enclose the structure entirely and then cut the framed windows and doorways.

Shingles

Take meticulous care to keep the edges of your shingles perfectly straight and level. Shingles last too long for you and your neighbors to endure a wavy or sloping pattern on your roof.

INDEX

METRIC CONVERSIONS

U.S. Units to Metric Equivalents			Metric Units to U.S. Equivalents		
To Convert From	Multiply By	To Get	To Convert From	Multiply By	To Get
Inches	25.4	Millimetres	Millimetres	0.0394	Inches
Inches	2.54	Centimetres	Centimetres	0.3937	Inches
Feet	30.48	Centimetres	Centimetres	0.0328	Feet
Feet	0.3048	Metres	Metres	3.2808	Feet
Yards	0.9144	Metres	Metres	1.0936	Yards
Square inches	6.4516	Square centimetres	Square centimetres	0.1550	Square inches
Square feet	0.0929	Square metres	Square metres	10.764	Square feet
Square yards	0.8361	Square metres	Square metres	1.1960	Square yards
Acres	0.4047	Hectares	Hectares	2.4711	Acres
Cubic inches	16.387	Cubic centimetres	Cubic centimetres	0.0610	Cubic inches
Cubic feet	0.0283	Cubic metres	Cubic metres	35.315	Cubic feet
Cubic feet	28.316	Litres	Litres	0.0353	Cubic feet
Cubic yards	0.7646	Cubic metres	Cubic metres	1.308	Cubic yards
Cubic yards	764.55	Litres	Litres	0.0013	Cubic yards

To convert from degrees Fahrenheit (F) to degrees Celsius (C), first subtract 32, then multiply by 5/9.

To convert from degrees Celsius to degrees Fahrenheit, multiply by 9/5, then add 32.